# Surrendering Hunger

# Surrendering Hunger

## 365 DEVOTIONS FOR CHRISTIANS RECOVERING FROM EATING DISORDERS

## Jan Johnson

HarperSanFrancisco
*A Division of HarperCollinsPublishers*

SURRENDERING HUNGER: *365 Devotions for Christians Recovering
from Eating Disorders.* Copyright © 1993
by Jan Johnson. All rights reserved. Printed in the United
States of America. No part of this book may be used or
reproduced in any manner whatsoever without written
permission except in the case of brief quotations embodied
in critical articles and reviews. For information address
HarperCollins *Publishers,* 10 East 53rd Street,
New York, NY 10022.

FIRST EDITION

Library of Congress Cataloging-in-Publication Data

Johnson, Jan.
    Surrendering hunger : 365 devotions for
Christians recovering from eating disorders /
Jan Johnson. — 1st ed.
        p.  cm.
    Includes index.
    ISBN 0-06-064251-3
    1. Eating disorders—Patients—Prayer-book and
devotions—English.  2. Devotional calendars.  I. Title.
    BV4910.35J64 1993                        92-54535
    242'.4—dc20                                    CIP

93 94 95 96 97 98 BANTA 10 9 8 7 6 5 4 3 2 1

This edition is printed on acid-free paper that meets the
American National Standards Institute Z39.48 Standard.

# Introduction

Those of us struggling with compulsive eating, compulsive dieting, bulimia, or anorexia know that working through these things is not a quick process. It doesn't happen in a week at a treatment center or in a month of going to support-group meetings. We work on these issues every day, several times a day.

The meditations in this book are designed to add strength and hope to the daily recovery experience of those struggling with any kind of eating disorder. I have based them on verses found throughout the Bible because my own recovery has awakened me spiritually to God as the loving parent presented there.

If you are unfamiliar with recovery wording, you may find the recovery words in the glossary helpful. If you're a little fuzzy on the spiritual-growth terms used, the glossary defines some of those, too. If perhaps you once had faith in God but now you're not sure, this book allows you to take a second look at faith and the nature of God's character.

I have used the masculine pronouns he, him, and his throughout this book to refer to God because adequate pronouns do not exist. The Bible says that God's image is both male and female (Genesis 1:27), so I believe that God's personhood is also both male and female. I regret limiting God by using only masculine pronouns, but I trust that "he" understands and I hope you do, too.

# *Do I Trust God?*

*And the Lord God commanded the man,
"You are free to eat from any tree in the
garden; but you must not eat from the tree of
the knowledge of good and evil, for when you
eat of it you will surely die."*—GENESIS 2:17

From the beginning, eating has been a problem for humans. But in the garden and even now the problem is much deeper. I'm not sure whom I trust and don't trust. My impression of God is so distorted that I don't trust him easily. Does he love me as I am? Does he value me in spite of my failures?

I have allowed other *powers* in this world to tell me what God is like. Teachers and friends valued outward actions instead of inward motivations; parents, being only human, did not portray the unconditional love of God. Part of recovering from an eating disorder is knowing God better and finding out what he's really like. As I do this, I can put my trust in him who, most of all, deserves my trust.

*Thank you, God, help me put my trust
in you and brush away all those other
images of you.*

The core issue is not my eating disorder,
but trusting God.

# I Didn't Do It!

*The man said, "The woman you put here*
*with me—she gave me some fruit*
*from the tree, and I ate it." . . . The woman*
*said, "The serpent deceived me, and I ate."*
—GENESIS 3:12

I have been like the man in this passage—putting the blame on someone else. I can take responsibility for my compulsive overeating, my short temper, and my laziness.

I see the destructive results of blaming others:

- blaming others distracts me from examining my own defects of character;

- blaming the same people over and over makes me dislike them more;

- blaming others keeps my life in an uproar; it robs me of any serenity I have.

For my own good, I stop blaming and start admitting when I'm wrong.

*God, help me recognize when I blame others,*
*and help me admit my own fault*
*in the matter.*

Time spent blaming is time wasted.

# *Releasing the Anger*

*Then the Lord said to Cain, "Why are you*
*angry? Why is your face downcast? . . .*
*[sin] desires to have you, but you must*
*master it."*—GENESIS 4:6–7

I'm like Cain when I'm angry. I try to bury my
anger and put on a happy face. But like Cain, my face
is downcast and I can't seem to shake it unless I work
through it. But that is too difficult, so I secretly numb
my anger by overeating or starving. Then I can put the
happy face back on for a while, although I never
know when my anger will leak.

God intervened to help Cain deal with his anger.
I often feel the same nudge from God myself. I'm
learning that when this happens I can work through
my anger in ways that don't hurt anyone else. I talk it
out with a friend or at a support group, I journal
about it, or I take one of my rather loud prayer walks.
Then I've released it and I'm free of my anger and my
need to overeat or starve.

*Thank you for prompting me*
*to surrender my anger to you.*

To admit and then let go of anger
is to find life, a day at a time.

## DAY 4

# *Purpose of Recovery*

*. . . and all peoples on earth will be blessed through you.* —GENESIS 12:3

Am I working on my eating disorder just so I can look good and impress others? Is my goal to have a nice life and not be a pain in the neck to anyone? Do I exist only to look within myself all day?

Yes, I need to look within myself, but also beyond myself. I see that God put me on earth to benefit other people. I tried to help others in the past, but my eating disorder handicapped me. I thought more about satisfying my neediness than how I could serve others. My prayers were pleas to relieve my neediness instead of inquiries about how I could follow God's will.

As I surrender my eating disorder, I rediscover God's purposes for my life because he teaches me how to get my needs met in healthy ways. I'm free to truly care about other people.

*God, help me see that my recovery isn't just to serve me, but to ultimately serve you.*

Self-improvement is never a big enough reason to change; fulfilling God's purposes is.

# *Shortcuts Can Get Me Lost*

> *Get rid of that slave woman and her son,*
> *for that slave woman's son will never share*
> *in the inheritance with my son Isaac.*
> —GENESIS 21:10

I want to feel better and look better, but I don't want to give up my eating disorder. Isn't there a shortcut? I wonder.

Abraham tried to take a shortcut to God's will by having a son, Ishmael, with a slave woman. When Ishmael made life miserable for Abraham's later son, Isaac (the son God intended Abraham to have), Ishmael had to leave.

My eating disorder is my Ishmael. It is my scheme to manage pain, feel better, and perform well in the chaos of life. But it is an unhealthy way to live, and I have to get rid of it.

Even though I may take the long way around to maintain a proper weight, I benefit so much from it. I find healthy ways to relate to God, others, and myself. I find my Isaac, God's true path for me.

*Once again, I give my compulsion to you and ask for healthier ways to deal with life.*

Daily I surrender my destructive
shortcuts to God.

# Does God Love Only the Good?

*. . . do not be afraid; God has heard the boy crying as he lies there. . . . Then God opened [Hagar's] eyes and she saw a well of water.*
—GENESIS 21:17, 19

Will God help me get out of this mess I've made? No, I don't deserve it.

But God helps those who mess up, too. Hagar was grieving and dying of thirst in the desert because she had made the worst of a bad situation. But God provided a well for her and her son. Even though she was more than partly at fault, he put the well there for her.

I am like Hagar. I am more than partly at fault for my eating disorder. I have isolated myself; I have tried to work it out on my own; I have misled others about my problem. Even though I am guilty of these things, God is still there for me. I don't have to be one hundred percent innocent for God to rescue me.

*God, I am grateful that you take care of me and meet my needs even when I mess up.*

God loves because he's faithful, not because I'm innocent.

## DAY 7

# *A Promise in Stone*

*This heap [of stones] is a witness, and this pillar is a witness, that I will not go past this heap to your side to harm you....*
—GENESIS 31:52–53

Are promises made to be broken? I have broken so many promises to myself to diet or to eat properly or to exercise more. I know the pain of broken promises.

One recovering manipulator, Jacob, and his enemy, Laban, set up a pile of stones to cement their promise not to harm each other. My friends who are struggling with an eating disorder (some of whom may be in my support group) become witnesses of what I commit myself to do and not do. I promise them that I will make an effort to start an abstinence (for more explanation, see glossary), make amends, or pray for someone I love to criticize. Their simple presence in my life, like the pile of stones, reminds me of my promise in a concrete way. If I fail, I have these human witnesses to forgive me and help me start over.

*Please give me the strength to use the powerful tool of accountability.*

Accountability is teamwork, and it puts more strength on my side.

# *Regret Reduction*

*So Jacob was left alone, and a man wrestled
with him till daybreak. When the man saw
that he could not overpower him, he touched
the socket of Jacob's hip so that his hip was
wrenched. . . . [Jacob] was limping because
of his hip.*—GENESIS 32:24–25, 31

Like others who have trafficked in eating disorders, I have done a miserable disservice to my body.
Like Jacob, I am limping. My metabolism is slowed so
that weight doesn't come off or stay off easily. My
junk-food eating has sped along my hypoglycemia.
These *limps* aren't endearing to me, but I don't regret
them either. They are memorials to the great battle I
am fighting. They hint at how much more damaged
I could be if I don't continue my recovery.

My battle wounds are signs that I am a seasoned
person who has acquired wisdom the hard way. I
have struggled with God, with others, with food, and
with a culture that worships food and thinness. I have
overcome because I have surrendered to God my val-
iant attempts to win the wrestling match with food.

*God, help me see my wounds as reminders
of how far I've come.*

I can live with the negative physical effects
of my eating disorder and not resent them
or beat myself up over them.

# DAY 9

# *Becoming Willing to Forgive*

*You intended to harm me, but God intended it for good to accomplish what is now being done....* —GENESIS 50:19–20

Surrender involves forgiving those who have intentionally harmed me. At first I may forgive because it's the smart thing to do. I know that if I hold grudges, I will eat compulsively or starve to relieve the bad feelings my grudges produce. So I give up my grudges to keep my abstinence.

As I progress in surrendering my eating disorder, I see why I'm so unwilling to forgive others: I don't trust God to keep me from further harm. In today's verses, Joseph trusted God and forgave his brothers because he could see how God's plan had worked to benefit everyone. Even if I can't see a master plan, I can trust the Master himself to reroute someone else's devious plan to my advantage. I surrender my bitterness, not because I trust the person I forgive, but because I trust God.

*Help me face my grudges and bitterness and turn them over to you, God.*

Today I trust God with my bitterness.

# When Their Faults Are My Faults

> . . . [Moses] killed the Egyptian and hid
> him. . . . The next day . . . he asked the one
> in the wrong, "Why are you hitting your
> fellow Hebrew?"—EXODUS 2:13

When I get upset with people, I'm often guilty of the same things they do. I don't like judgmental people, but I judge quickly. I don't like grumpy people, but I can be grumpy. When I haven't worked out a problem in my own life, I spot it easily in others' lives—much like Moses who tried to break up a fight the day after he had murdered someone!

To truly surrender my eating disorder I have to quit taking inventories of other people's faults. I take responsibility for my own faults instead. I ask God to show me what I need to do to become abstinent and grow spiritually.

The only person I should try to change is myself, so I get on with it and let God take care of others.

*God, show me my character defects*
*and help me release them to you.*

I will be able to help others more when
I have faced my own faults.

## DAY 11

# *Scared to Step Out*

*But Moses said, "O Lord, please send
someone else to do it."*—EXODUS 4:13

It's scary to pay attention to the promptings of
God, and it's scary to ignore them. My love for my eating behaviors tells me to ignore God's promptings
because they get in the way of my getting what I feel
I need most—food.

As my abstinence drowns out the thunder of my
compulsion, God's promptings seem louder. Sometimes I feel as if I'm standing in front of a burning
bush, saying, "God, please ask someone else to start
a support group . . . or to volunteer at the street
mission."

As I face my fear and wait and pray, God plants
a desire within me that is stronger than the fear. So I
take the plunge. When I follow God's prompting (not
my own grandiose desire for applause), it's more
rewarding than I could have imagined.

*God, help me listen to your promptings
and follow them.*

To follow God's promptings is to enjoy
the little excitements of life.

# DAY 12

## *Tools I Don't Understand*

*Take a bunch of hyssop, dip it into the blood in the basin and put some of the blood on the top and on both sides of the door frame.*—EXODUS 12:22

If I had been an Israelite hearing the instructions in today's verse, I would have said, "Forget it. That's a disgusting idea." Of course, I've thought that becoming abstinent, attending support groups, and making telephone calls were ridiculous, too. When I'm ready to practice my compulsion, few helpful ideas make sense to me.

Yet I see what the Israelites could not see—that the blood above and to the sides of the door frame form the three upper points of the cross of Christ. In a sense, the Israelites were calling on the power of Christ by putting blood on their door frames. And as I practice abstinence, attend my support group, and make telephone calls, I'm turning over my hunger and my need to control to Christ. I need his power to help me.

*Help me to use the proven tools of abstinence, support groups, and telephone calls to surrender to you even though their importance eludes me.*

To do is to understand.

# *Serenity in Stillness*

*The Lord will fight for you; you need
only be still.*—EXODUS 14:14

If I am going to stop overeating or starving, I have
to stop panicking, too. As a compulsive controller,
I move into the panic mode when a crisis strikes.

No more. Now I take care of what is within my
control, knowing that most things in life are not
within my control. Often I'm trapped like the Israelites were between a powerful Egyptian army and the
Red Sea. I am learning to trust that God is going to
part that Red Sea—without my interference.

When I am confident that God will intervene,
I have serenity. Others may urge me to panic, to plot,
and to coerce, but I "need only be still." Finally, I am
learning to watch and wait for God to part the Red
Seas in my life.

*Thank you, God, that you invade impossible
situations and give me the serenity I need.*

To wait and be still
is an unexplainable serenity.

# God's Learning Curve

*The Lord is my strength and my song; he has become my salvation.*—EXODUS 15:2

I thought I knew God. Yet as I work on abstaining from my eating-disorder behaviors, I lean on God as never before. He becomes my strength.

I also thank God for my progress even though it is slow. I celebrate with him in prayer and in the way I report to my struggling friends. He becomes my song.

As I examine my character defects and allow God to permeate every area of my life, no matter how disgusting, I become fully identified with him. He's becoming my daily salvation in everything I do.

*God, please come into my life
in a greater way.*

Leaning on God is how it begins;
identifying with him is how it continues.

# Recovery Fills Me Up

*Thin flakes like frost on the ground appeared*
*on the desert floor. When the Israelites saw it,*
*they said to each other, "What is it?"*
—EXODUS 16:14–15

As I practice abstinence, I look at the food on my plate as if it were manna and say, "What is it?" The sight of five ounces of broccoli is a strange sight. Have I traded in my compulsive overeating, my chocolate binges, and my controlled starvation for this? It isn't much of a prize.

This is the stark reality of abstinence. I have turned my back on food. It can no longer be a soothing friend or a weapon for control. It is only a nourishing substance.

If I were on a diet, this healthy food might make me grouchy, but true recovery from an eating disorder is different. I fill my life with prayer, meditation, reading, and serving others. I am finally involved in worthwhile activities that do not involve overconsuming or underconsuming food!

*God, help me shift my focus from food to life.*

I used to live to eat; now I eat to live.

# Meeting with God

*Then Moses led the people out of the camp to meet with God, and they stood at the foot of the mountain.*—EXODUS 19:17

At regular intervals, I meet with God. Yes, it's difficult to go "out of the camp" of my daily life for a few minutes or hours, but it's so rewarding when I do.

I don't expect fireworks or great revelations from my time with God. I expect only to meet God in some way, and because he's such a varied being, I meet him in various ways. I hear him talk through the Scripture, through my meditation on it, through my own journaling and prayers, and through the stillness of being with him.

I come away knowing that I am loved by God, knowing that I am no longer useless because he has great designs for me.

*Thank you for meeting with me, God, and letting me know that I am loved.*

Meeting with God becomes something I look forward to.

# Can Good Come Out of Anger?

*When Moses approached the camp and saw the calf and the dancing, his anger burned and he threw the tablets out of his hands, breaking them to pieces. . . .*—EXODUS 32:19

Anger is like fire. It can be used for good purposes when it motivates us to right wrongs. But too often I express my righteous anger in unhealthy ways. Like Moses, I may have good reasons to be angry, but I hurt the people I love the most. That's why I tried to cover up my anger with compulsive overeating and starving.

If I'm to surrender these behaviors, I have to look at my anger and make choices about it. When people and situations frustrate me, I can allow the passion stirred within me to motivate me to do something constructive instead of destructive. I can calm myself and say or do something helpful. My anger can do some good, as fire warms a cold world.

*Take my anger, Lord, and use it in a positive way.*

When I give my anger to God, great things happen.

# Being Versus Doing

*The Lord replied, "My Presence will go with you, and I will give you rest."*—EXODUS 33:14

In the past, I thought God wanted me to be up and doing every minute. I frantically tried to figure out how to please him, and I did and did and did.

I've come to see that God loves me and sees me as something more than a machine. He not only encourages me to rest, but he gives me rest. As I acknowledge his continuous presence in my life, I can abide in his rest and taste some of that serenity I've been chasing. I refuel so that in the fray of battle, I am more reassured and less panicked.

*Thank you, God, for helping me learn to rest in your presence.*

God wants me to "be" with him; he will lead me to the proper amount of doing.

# Moving Beyond Failures

*The Lord said to Moses, "Chisel out two stone tablets like the first ones, and I will write on them the words that were on the first tablets, which you broke."*—EXODUS 34:1

When I make mistakes, no one judges me more harshly than I judge myself. To me, mistakes aren't something I can correct, but catastrophes I must regret for the rest of my life. That's one reason I feel such a need to overeat and to control my overeating.

I marvel at how God forgave Moses for breaking the stones on which the Ten Commandments were written and simply told him to write them again. I want to be that kind of parent to myself and to my children. When I fall flat on my face, I want to get up, brush myself off, and say, "Let's try again."

Even if I should break my abstinence, I want to talk to recovering friends that same day and say, "God is helping me begin again."

*Thank you, God, for picking up the pieces of myself and letting me start over.*

Failure doesn't have to defeat me unless
I beat myself up over it.

# *Others May, I Cannot*

*You must not do as they do in Egypt, where
you used to live, and you must not do as they
do in the land of Canaan, where I am
bringing you. Do not follow their
practices.*—LEVITICUS 18:3

It feels as if everyone around me is stuffing themselves on sugary foods or talking about losing weight and skipping meals. They don't seem to have any problems. Couldn't I just this once do the same thing. . . .

I know what I need to do: to adopt a sane, healthy eating plan in my life and to grow in the light God has given me. It doesn't matter if my culture is food-oriented or my friends overeat or diet incessantly. I now know I am important to God and to others in my support group. I will not overeat, overdiet, overspend, or oversex even though my culture says this compulsive behavior is normal behavior.

*Help me, God, know and love you so well
that your voice blocks out the voices of
compulsion in my culture.*

Others may follow my culture,
but I choose not to do so.

# *Progress I Don't Understand*

> *Five of you will chase a hundred, and a
> hundred of you will chase ten thousand,
> and your enemies will fall by the sword
> before you.*—LEVITICUS 26:7–8

As difficult as recovering from an eating disorder can be, there are small improvements that I can't explain.

I struggle so long with chocolate and turn down one candy bar and suddenly all kinds of food have less appeal for me. I focus on quieting my voice with my children and it seems hopeless, but then I find I'm less frustrated with my co-workers. I progress when I'm not looking, and I can't explain why.

That's the beauty of it. With God, five soldiers can defeat one hundred soldiers. If I could explain it, I would claim I won in my strength and feel proud, then I would fall. This way, I can only report my progress to my recovering friends and celebrate with them. These small moments of grace become inside jokes with God.

> *Work in me, using your mysterious paths,
> God, and I promise to cooperate.*

God's ways are mysterious, and that's OK.

# My Conscience, My Friend

*When a man or woman wrongs another . . .
that person is guilty and must confess
the sin he has committed. He must make
full restitution for his wrong. . . .*
—NUMBERS 5:6–7

When I have a guilty conscience, I try to ignore it but I still feel needy inside. Neediness stirs up my drivenness, and I want to overeat, purge, or starve.

If I'm to abstain from these behaviors, I have to confess my faults, ask forgiveness, and make amends. It isn't pleasant to face people and situations I would rather forget, but it cleanses me. I'm able to live with myself without the numbing effect of food.

Asking forgiveness and making amends sets a pattern of taking responsibility for my hurtful actions. The next time I think about doing something hurtful, my conscience awakens and pleads with me, "Please don't make me confess and make restitution again! Anything but that!" So I change my path and do what seems to be the kindest, most helpful thing.

*God, please give me the courage to confess
my mistakes and make amends.*

A clean conscience decreases my need
for my eating disorder.

# When Griping Grips Me

*Now the people complained about their
hardships in the hearing of the Lord, and
when he heard them his anger was
aroused.*—NUMBERS 11:1

Griping is often a well-developed hobby for
compulsives. Take me anywhere and I can come up
with five things that are wrong with any person,
place, or thing. The more I gripe, the more I feel the
need to manage and control.

So griping becomes one more thing I confess to
my support group. I can try a simple accountability
such as not complaining for twenty-four hours. The
next night and next day I catch myself with my mouth
open, ready to spew forth cranky complaints, but
nothing comes out. When people say, "What were
you going to say?" I can smile.

Changing my behavior this way is difficult but
wonderful. Life is so much better. I do this as often as
I need to until I find that I feel more grateful all the
time.

*Thank you, Lord, that while you help me
process my thoughts and feelings you also
help me break bad habits.*

My hopelessness fades
as my complaining fades.

# Better Off Where?

*The Lord heard you when you wailed,*
*"If only I had meat to eat! We were better off*
*in Egypt!"*—NUMBERS 11:18

When I long to return to my eating-disorder behaviors, I don't know what I'm asking for. I resemble
the Israelites who became tired of eating manna every
day. Their appetites were so distorted that they said
they were better off in Egypt as slaves making bricks
because sometimes they got meat to eat.

I have the same choice. I can choose slavery or
freedom. In the days when my compulsion drives me,
much of my life is clouded by my appetite. I choose
social activities based on whether or not food is
served; I choose friends who also overeat or starve; I
make the rounds of convenience stores for junk food.
Now I'm free to choose jobs, friendships, and social
activities with no thought of how close they take me
to an ice cream parlor.

*God, show me just how much my eating*
*disorder enslaves me.*

I'm better off without the enslavement
of my eating disorder.

# *What Humility Isn't*

*Now Moses was a very humble man,
more humble than anyone else on the face
of the earth.*—NUMBERS 12:3

Humility is important in surrendering an eating disorder, but what does humility mean?

Does it mean I can't make decisions? No, Moses decided (with God's direction) to lead a nation out of slavery.

Does it mean I never feel anger? No, Moses was rightfully angry when the Israelites worshiped a golden calf.

Does it mean I'm always afraid—or never afraid? Neither. Moses was reluctant to lead the Israelites, but he did it after he was convinced that God would supply the power.

Humility means that I put God in charge of public relations. I don't have to impress anyone or compare myself to anyone to feel better about myself. I can be me and let God take care of the rest.

*God, I give you my worries about how I look
and who likes me.*

Humility means self-forgetfulness instead
of self-obsession.

# *Trusting As I Go*

*But the men who had gone up with him said,
"We can't attack those people; they are
stronger than we are."*—NUMBERS 13:31

My eating disorder has been my comfort zone.
The thought of abstinence sometimes seems too
scary to pursue. Like the men in today's verse who
were afraid to take possession of their promised land,
I claim, "I can't attack my eating disorder. It's stronger
than I am."

But it isn't stronger. These men were afraid and
exaggerated the obstacles. So do I.

I need only a small amount of trust—only
enough to step out and go to a support group. As I
move along, my trust in God grows to fit the increasing risks—taking an inventory, making amends, and
becoming abstinent.

Each risk stretches me enough to take the next
step.

*God, please help me let go of my insatiable
need for safety and cling to your protection.*

Only by going out on a limb can I get
to the fruit.

# God Defends Me

*But the whole assembly talked about stoning them. Then the glory of the Lord appeared at the Tent of Meeting to all the Israelites.*
—NUMBERS 14:10

What do I do when people stone me with words even though I am innocent? Moses and Aaron did nothing and waited for God to display his presence and power. I am learning that there's a difference between honest seekers who want to understand me and quick condemners who want to blame me. Some criticism is helpful; some is not.

If the criticism isn't helpful, it's useless to defend myself. Offering a calm logical defense does not diffuse the anger of my accusers. In fact, it often inflames it further.

As I improve my conscious contact with God, I try to follow his guidance concerning the times I should defend myself and the times I should be silent and let God defend me.

*Please, God, give me the serenity to avoid making exhausting defenses when it will do no good.*

God rules, and I will be exonerated at the appropriate time.

# *God's Balanced Character*

*The Lord is slow to anger, abounding
in love and forgiving sin and rebellion.
Yet he does not leave the guilty
unpunished.*—NUMBERS 14:18

Many people see God as:

- all justice: a punishing tyrant
- all mercy: a permissive, pushover parent.

The idea that God can be just and merciful at the same time is paradoxical, but real. I understand it only as I practice it. God can work in my life when I admit I'm a compulsive eater and I make amends (justice), but also when I forgive myself (mercy).

This balance of justice and mercy spreads through my life as I'm more eager to be fair yet forgiving when I clear up misunderstandings with a friend. Those days of harshness one day and permissiveness the next are fading, and I'm finding the balance I've needed for a long time.

*Thanks you, God, for being just and merciful,
fair yet forgiving.*

Mercy without justice produces
sentimentality; justice without mercy
produces legalism. Justice and mercy
together produce genuineness.

# Presenting My Anger to God

*Then Moses became very angry and said
to the Lord, "Do not accept their offering.
I have not . . . wronged any of them."*
—NUMBERS 16:15

Can I hide my anger from God? I sure try. Sometimes I try so hard to hide it from others, too, that I end up unleashing it when I least expect it.

Like Moses though, I can take my anger to God. I can lay out the problem before him. In this process, I sometimes discover that I am at fault, then I go to the person I offended and make amends. Other times, I am angry for a good reason as Moses was.

By presenting my anger to God, I am taking it to the only person who can do anything about it. God can calm me. He can also correct or change my opponent in ways I can't. With God's help, I can release the anger.

*God, thank you for loving me when
I'm angry, accepting my anger, and helping
me resolve it.*

I trust God enough to show him my hurts
instead of hiding them from him.

# *Blaming God*

*They spoke against God and against Moses,
and said, "Why have you brought us
up out of Egypt to die in the desert?"*
—NUMBERS 21:5

As my eating disorder progressed, I felt hopeless.
Nothing worked and I developed a bitterness toward
God. In my most frustrated moments, I prayed, "Why
aren't you helping me, God?" I blamed God because
I was on the wrong path.

Now that I'm surrendering this problem to God,
I recognize my tendency to blame him for things.
My problem is similar to the Israelites' problem. I am
on the right path, but it's longer and harder than
I thought it would be. It's easy to accuse God of
deceiving me and breaking his promises.

So when I start accusing, I stop. I ask myself if
I'm creating this problem through my own unhealthy
behavior. Or am I growing impatient with myself,
even though God is patient with me?

*God, I admit my bitterness toward you and
ask for your forgiveness and healing.*

Bitterness hardens my heart; surrender
nourishes hope.

## DAY 31

# *I Have Enough*

> *. . . you shall not set your desire on your neighbor's house or land . . . his ox or donkey, or anything that belongs to your neighbor.*—DEUTERONOMY 5:21

I used to think everyone else had it better. One friend had a better marriage, another had a better car, and they all had a better life. When I think this way, I'm saying that God doesn't know what he's doing, that he hasn't given me what I need to make it in life, and that what he provides for me will never be enough, or at least good enough.

Gratefulness changes my attitude. I can be grateful for God's unconditional love and that he chooses to delight in me—no matter what I weigh, no matter how I look. I can be grateful that he has given me everything I need to survive and to grow in my recovery. I can even be grateful for people I know who have acquired more than I have.

*God, I am grateful that you have supplied exactly what I need for today.*

Whatever God provides is enough for me today.

# Good, Better, or Best?

*Love the Lord your God with all your heart
and with all your soul and with all your
strength.*—DEUTERONOMY 6:5

There are so many *good* things to seek. I can seek happiness, I can seek health, I can seek a good marriage, but they will never be enough to fill the empty space inside me. Seeking God and loving him with everything I've got is the only thing that will be enough.

Yet I still find myself focusing on the extras. When I weigh the right amount, I'll be able to wear more of my clothes. Without that distraction of food, I'll be able to perform better on my job than ever before. With all the patience I'm learning, I'll be the best co-worker I've ever been.

All those things are good, but they aren't the very best. And they are never reason enough to recover from an eating disorder. The best reason to surrender this disorder is to know God better and find my place in doing his will.

*God, help me move beyond good motives
for working through this eating disorder.*

To seek God is to find life.

# Will My Progress Continue?

*When the Lord your God brings you into
the land . . . be careful that you do not
forget the Lord, who brought you out of
Egypt, out of the land of slavery.*
—DEUTERONOMY 6:10–12

Success doesn't have to be a spoiler. With whatever progress I experience (including months and years of abstinence), I have a choice. I can use that progress to move on, or I can use it to slide, thinking that I've done something about my problem and can now coast.

On the contrary, I bring my progress before God, my sponsor, and my support group, and we celebrate it together. I can get the affirmation I need. I can avoid that rebellious part of me that runs ahead of myself and ruins things, and then snickers, What made you think things would ever go well for you?

It's time to lay down those old attitudes of laziness and spoiling. I can take up serenity and peace.

*Thank you, God, for my progress,
however small it may be, and help me hang
on to it when I get discouraged.*

Affirmation can spur me on.

## DAY 34

# *Compromising My Abstinence*

*Make no treaty with them, and show them no mercy.*—DEUTERONOMY 7:2

Sure, I said that I would eat three meals a day, but I can't sleep without a bedtime snack. Or I binge on chips and dip and call it a meal. Or I sense that God is working overtime by the way the drive-through lines are so long and the convenience store is out of my binge food, but I make a treaty with the enemy and drive miles out of my way to get the food I *need*. I don't trust God's power to get me through my neediness.

One of the deceits of an eating disorder is that I think tomorrow will bring another opportunity to become abstinent or to refine my abstinence. I can start then. Perhaps, but perhaps not. As I grow more desperate, I see that others have given up completely and that I could easily do the same if I don't seize my opportunity now.

*Give me, Lord, the desperation I need to use every opportunity to recover from my disordered behaviors.*

No more treaties with the enemy.

# God Is Trustworthy

> *Know therefore that the Lord your God is
> God; he is the faithful God, keeping his
> covenant of love to a thousand generations
> of those who love him and keep him
> commands.*—DEUTERONOMY 7:9

Part of the reason I trust my compulsion is that I don't trust anything or anyone else. I might have been significantly disappointed by family members; I might have leaned too hard on friends; I might have expected the world to grant me favors. I might have prayed and asked God to deliver me, and it seemed that even God disappointed me.

Now I'm learning that God is trustworthy; "He is the faithful God." No, he doesn't deliver a magic abstinence, instant friends, or immediate serenity. But when I lay my needs before him, he doesn't let me down. When I follow his path, he clears the way before me.

*God, help me know you as the faithful and
trustworthy being you are, even when I don't
understand what's going on.*

To trust God is to come to know him
and feel loved by him.

# The Unhurried Recovery

*The Lord your God will drive out those nations before you, little by little. You will not be allowed to eliminate them all at once, or the wild animals will multiply around you.* —DEUTERONOMY 7:21–22

I have often wished that God would instantly, miraculously transform me into an angelic person with stable emotions, tamed inner drives, and perfect behavior. Then I would have no problems and no eating disorder.

But just as God moved the Israelites slowly into their promised land, he moves me slowly through the growing process.

My setbacks and struggles are not lost moments. As long as I'm making progress, I'm claiming new territory. Little by little, I can express my emotions in more appropriate ways.

This slow, steady progress keeps the "wild animals" away. I don't transfer my obsessiveness to compulsive spending, sexual fantasies, or workaholic highs to manage the pain I used to let my eating disorder manage. I give it all up.

*Thank you, God, for the small amount of progress each day, even when I can't see it.*

God sets the pace of my journey.

# *Using All the Tools*

> *Be careful to follow every command I am*
> *giving you today, so that you may live*
> *and increase and may enter and possess*
> *the land that the Lord promised. . . .*
> —DEUTERONOMY 8:1

Because I still have to eat to live, it's easy to have a half-baked recovery from an eating disorder. I feel myself trying to pretend I'm not angry so I don't have to write about it in my journal or talk to a friend about it or pray about it. I say that my abstinence is important, but I watch my food portions get a little too big or small.

The journey of surrendering an eating disorder is a lot like the Israelites' quest to possess the promised land. They had to be freed from the Egyptians, they had to cross the Red Sea, and they had to wander. I have Red Seas to cross and wanderings to endure. I can't neglect any of the footwork.

I want to fully possess the promised land of recovery, so I'm going to follow every command every day and use every tool. The tools that make me squirm are usually the ones I need the most. When I use all of them, recovery is a rich place to be.

*Thank you, God, for the tools that help me*
*"possess the land." Help me not to neglect*
*any of them.*

The tools I fear using are the ones
I need to use.

# *Feeding on the Truth*

*He humbled you, causing you to hunger and
then feeding you with manna ... to teach
you that man does not live on bread alone
but on every word that comes from the
mouth of the Lord.* —DEUTERONOMY 8:3

My abstinence causes me to hunger physically
for food and emotionally for control. When these
hungers flare up, I can choose not to feed on food or
the starvation from it, but on manna, the godly principles of God:

- God loves me;
- God sees my value when others around me do
  not;
- God is working in me to bring out positive
  qualities and capabilities in me I never thought
  were possible.

In spite of my disappointments, my frustrations,
and my anger, I accept the truth of these principles.
Slowly they become part of me through prayer, journaling, meditation, and service.

*Teach me, God, to depend on you instead
of on my eating disorder.*

Seeking God fills my
inner and outer hunger.

# The Plentiful Land
# of Recovery

*For the Lord your God is bringing you into a
good land . . . a land where bread will not be
scarce and you will lack nothing.*
—DEUTERONOMY 8:7, 9

It is tempting to view abstinence as a dry land of
nothingness because I can't overeat or plot ways to
become thin. But it is not a barren land, but an exciting, prosperous one.

As I adjust to a normal level of hunger, I discover
that I lack nothing. So much fills my life because I am
facing my defects of character. Because I'm learning
how to handle my jealousy and fear of intimacy,
my relationships are improving. Because I'm not so
afraid of failure, my daily tasks are becoming interesting puzzles. I'm forgiving others and releasing the
problems of my past. I'm making new and better
goals because I see my value and believe in myself. I
feel inner fulfillment because I am confident that
God loves me no matter how much I weigh.

*Help me to trust that recovery
is a better place in life.*

Life can be filled with all the good things
I missed when I was obsessed with food
and thinness.

# Opening My Hand to Others

*If there is a poor man among your
brothers . . . be openhanded and freely
lend him whatever he needs.*
—DEUTERONOMY 15:7–8

There is a panicky tightfistedness about an eating disorder. I can't let go of my food or the money I need to buy the food. Because I've become so preoccupied with myself, I feel insecure and squelch any generous feelings I may have.

As I surrender this eating disorder, I feel so grateful to God and to my recovering friends that I loosen my grip a little on life. I find I'm a little more openhanded. I handle money better. I'm more touched by the needs of others, and I want to share my resources more with the needy. I become as excited about giving as receiving.

*God, please use me as an instrument
of your openhandedness.*

Generosity grows out of gratefulness.

# *Changing from Within*

*Do not let this Book of the Law depart from
your mouth; meditate on it day and night, so
that you may be careful to do everything
written in it.*—JOSHUA 1:8

My old fears and negative attitudes linger. Could
I have them surgically removed, or would I change if
I ripped out Bible pages and ate them in a sandwich?

No, but I can meditate. I can read a verse or two
of Scripture, close my eyes, and ask myself a few
questions:

- What difference does this verse make to me?

- What would I do if I were to put this into
  action?

- What is God trying to get through to me?

As I absorb the verses and wait, interesting
things happen. Sometimes I sense a rush of feeling—
a release of anger or frustration. Other times I get an
idea about something I should do. Still other times
nothing happens. But always I thank God for his
abiding presence, and that is enough.

*As I meditate on your words, God,
help me to be renewed.*

Meditation penetrates beyond the mind
into the will and the heart.

# *Celebrating My Progress!*

*[Joshua] said to the Israelites, "In the future when your descendants ask their fathers, 'What do these stones mean?' tell them, 'Israel crossed the Jordan on dry ground.'"*
—JOSHUA 4:21–22

The Israelites built memorials to recall their victories and defeats. I have some memorials, too. They include:

- a bent and yellowed recipe card for chocolate cheesecake that I used to make often and well;
- a half shelf of diet books that now read like a foreign language to me;
- a stained, baggy sweatshirt I used to cover up overweight and underweight;
- journals full of recovering true confessions;
- the first recovery book I read full of red underlining and exclamation points—with potato chip crumbs in the seam.

These mementos remind me of how far I've progressed and the bondage from which I've escaped.

*Help me, God, not to forget how far I've come, no matter how far that is or isn't.*

I am becoming a different person.

# *Procrastinating*

*So Joshua said to the Israelites: "How long
will you wait before you begin to take
possession of the land that the Lord, the God
your fathers, has given you?"*—JOSHUA 18:3

"I have to wait until I'm in a better place in
life . . . to try abstinence; to write my inventory; to
refine my abstinence."

When I say these words, am I waiting for a better
life or a fantastic life? It is not going to come.

If I regret anything about recovery, it's that I
waited so long to begin it, that I stalled so long on plateaus, that I haven't used the tools more often. While
I stood in the waiting rooms (and perhaps some of
that waiting was necessary), I hurt myself and many
other people. I cannot take that back, but I can remain serious about my progress today.

*Thank you, God, for my progress, and nudge
me out of my waiting rooms.*

To put off growth is to put off having
a better life.

# Doubts and Questions

*"But sir," said Gideon, "if the Lord is with us,*
*why has all this happened to us? Where are*
*all his wonders that our fathers told us*
*about. . . ."*—JUDGES 6:13

Can you imagine asking an angel of the Lord the
questions Gideon asked? Most people think it's
wrong to question God as Gideon did, but God
(through the angel) told Gideon, "Go in the strength
you have. . . ." (v. 14). Then God commissioned Gideon
to save Israel. Apparently, God didn't think Gideon
was wrong to ask questions.

As abstinence causes my buried feelings to surface, I need to get all my cards of confusion, doubt,
and bitterness on the table and examine them. Am I
mad at God? Do I doubt his love for me? Where was
he during my childhood trauma?

I may not get answers I fully understand by
5:00 P.M. the same day, and I don't have to. But I do
need to present them to him. Then he can answer
them in his timing, and I know I'm accepted by the
one I desperately need.

*Lord, I love you, but I get frustrated*
*with the way things happen. Show me how*
*to resolve that.*

I can feel safe enough with God
to question him.

# *How Sponsors Help*

> *But Ruth replied, "Don't urge me to leave you or to turn back from you. Where you go I will go, and where you stay I will stay. Your people will be my people and your God my God."*—RUTH 1:16

As a young widow, Ruth no doubt felt broken and aimless. She followed the comings and goings of her mother-in-law, in spite of their religious and cultural gaps. She even adopted Naomi's faith.

This is similar to what happens between sponsors and those they sponsor. By asking a sponsor to help me, I am saying:

- Show me how to start over.
- Show me how to mend my brokenness.
- Help me break out of my isolation.
- Show me that you accept me.
- Show me how your faith works.
- Warn me if I get off track.

As I sponsor others, I have the honor of doing these things.

> *Help me choose a sponsor and learn all I can from that relationship.*

A sponsor shows me what the recovering life is like.

# Rooting Out the Pain

*. . . Hannah replied, "I am a woman who is
deeply troubled. I have not been drinking
wine or beer; I was pouring out my soul to
the Lord."*—1 SAMUEL 1:15

Hannah responded to the pain of childlessness
by pouring out her soul to the Lord. She prayed with
such feeling that the priest thought she was drunk.
What a healthy release for grief and frustration.

The same frustrations that drive me to overeat
and compulsively diet drive me to pour out my soul
to the Lord. As I pray this way, I release instead of
hoarding; I feel, instead of numbing out; I touch
someone, instead of withdrawing; I know his presence, instead of my own loneliness.

*God, I want to be willing to show my true
self to you without shame or embarrassment.*

I can trust God enough to pour out
my soul to him.

# *Brokenness Gives Life*

*The Lord brings death and makes alive; he
brings down to the grave and raises up.*
—1 SAMUEL 2:6

I welcome my pain and desperation because
they force me to examine myself and come clean.
They bring forth life.

I feel so miserable that I gather up my courage,
set aside my pride, and admit to someone else that I
have been dishonest and conceited. Then this person
thanks me, saying "You have named my problem for
me. I see it all now and I want to change, just like you
said." This person's brokenness speaks to mine and
we are a team. We form a strong friendship and continue to share our stories.

I'm glad I've surrendered to this death of myself.
Without it, I would not have found life.

*Help me, God, to accept your way of bringing
me new life from my brokenness.*

I can admit my brokenness in many ways
without shame.

# *Principles Before Personalities*

*But when they said, "Give us a king to lead us," this displeased Samuel; so he prayed to the Lord.*—1 SAMUEL 8:6

When I let my behavior hinge on one person ("a king to lead us"), I place personalities before principles. This happens when I let my abstinence become wrapped up in a sponsor, friend, or therapist. If they fail me or are no longer available for some reason, I break my abstinence.

Recovering from an eating disorder is based on the principles of God and God himself. I surrender to God, not to someone else. I get through tough times of abstinence because God provides me with help through others and through tools I use by myself such as prayer, meditation, Scripture reading, and journaling. I establish and strengthen my relationship with God. It is God who sustains me and can never fail me.

*Help me, God, not to lean too heavily on others or allow their mistakes to create problems for me.*

I can separate my choice to abstain from the successes and failures of others.

# No Longer Hiding

*You have done this evil; yet do not turn
away from the Lord, but serve the Lord with
all your heart.*—1 SAMUEL 12:20

It's tough to go back to a support group after I've broken my abstinence; it's tough to admit to anyone that I've exaggerated; it's tough to pray after I've blown up at my kids. I think God (and probably everyone else) is disgusted with me because I goofed.

When I want to run and hide, I need to come out and show my face. God may or may not be disgusted with me, but he still loves me and wants me to turn to him. The others will handle it the best they can.

I'm learning to stand up instead of hide and to get those unbearable moments over with when I'd like to put them off indefinitely. The results are usually not as bad as I imagine them to be, and I find a sense of healing from owning up to my faults and starting over.

*Help me, God, to learn to come to you
when I goof.*

When I want to hide from God,
I need him the most.

# Achieving Importance

> ... the Lord has sought out a man after his
> own heart and appointed him leader of his
> people, because you have not kept the Lord's
> command.—1 SAMUEL 13:14

My culture convinces me that I cannot be outstanding or influential unless I am good-looking,
well-educated, or highly skilled. King Saul was at
least two of these. He was physically appealing (a
head taller than others) and a brave, successful war-
rior. Why would God replace this statuesque man with
David, an unknown keeper of smelly sheep? Saul
lacked something important that David the shepherd
had: David was a man after God's own heart.

In the past, I felt ineffective no matter how hard
I tried or how good I looked. I was never good enough.
Now I no longer care about being outstanding or
influential; I want to seek after God, and I trust that
he gives me whatever significance and influence he
wants me to have.

*I seek after you, God. I no longer concern
myself with being outstanding and
influential.*

It's what I seek in life, not how I look, that
gives me significance.

# *Surviving Rejection*

*Then the word of the Lord came to Samuel:
"I am grieved that I have made Saul king,
because he has turned away from me and
has not carried out my instructions."*
—1 SAMUEL 15:10

Even God gets rejected. When Saul passed over God, God grieved, but he also moved on, asking Samuel to appoint another king.

I'm learning that I can choose how I wish to respond to being dismissed. I don't have to assume that others think I'm a worthless person. I don't have to jump on my high horse and scorn the other person forever.

Like God, I can grieve and go on. I may understand the rejection better as time passes. I may see how I unintentionally hurt that person, or I may learn that their objections had little to do with me and everything to do with things they were going through. And when I am at fault, I can choose to learn from my mistakes.

*God, help me get through rejection and
go on. Help me not take it personally.*

Rejection doesn't have to cripple me.

# Mood-Swing Mania

*To obey is better than sacrifice.*
—1 SAMUEL 15:22

"Let me make it up to you!" I used to say. As long as I was following the dictates of my eating disorder and living in my feelings, I found it impossible to be kind on a regular basis. It was much easier to withdraw or to be harsh or hypersensitive. I said a lot of things I didn't mean. Then when my negative mood was over, I was ready to make it up to whomever I'd harmed.

Nothing replaces simply being kind in the first place. No one enjoyed my emotional roller coasters. Now I find that I don't enjoy them either.

I'd much rather *obey* by straightening out my attitude now, so I don't have to *sacrifice* by worrying about how I'll make it up to someone for being so unkind, grouchy, or lazy.

*God, live in me and through me so I can*
*learn to be kind on a regular basis.*

Preventing a bad mood works better than
making up for one.

# Looks Can Be Defeating

*Man looks at the outward appearance, but the Lord looks at the heart.*—1 SAMUEL 16:7

My outward appearance has been the downer in my life for a long time. I was never thin enough; when I weighed the right amount, I was never proportioned correctly; even when I thought I looked good, my face was such an odd shape!

As I move through recovery, my belief that God loves me grows; this helps me accept my body, my face, and my normal shape (even though some would say the last item resembles a pear). There are still days when no matter how skillfully I apply makeup and how deftly I work with my hair, I don't look good enough to suit myself. So I remind myself that I'm OK. I lean forward and whisper to the face in the mirror, "Hello, world. This is me. This face is as good as it's going to get, and that's OK! OK?"

*Steep me in your love and all the nurturing that it brings, and let it soak through to my flagging self-esteem.*

Because God looks on my heart with mercy, I can learn to look at my outward appearance with mercy.

# Living in the Extremes

*Is that why you have all conspired against me? No one tells me. . . . None of you. . . .*
—1 SAMUEL 22:8

These extreme words—all, no one, none—were the words of a near madman, King Saul, who slaughtered the people to whom he spoke these words. The compulsive tendency is toward all or nothing, black or white.

I am learning to think and do things in moderation, which feels uncomfortable at first. I don't have to binge or starve. No matter how much I adore people, they are not one hundred percent wonderful. Carbohydrates aren't bad—they're part of a balanced diet.

Moderation is full of paradoxes! There is some good in the worst of us and some bad in the best of us. I don't have to rage; I can be moderately angry and cope with it. I don't have to panic or withdraw; I can stay with my uneasiness and let it pass.

*Thank you, Lord, for leading me away from the extreme paths in life.*

I don't have to live out on the edge anymore; I can enjoy balance and moderation in life.

# *Stormy Relationships*

*Some urged me to kill you, but I spared you;*
*I said, "I will not lift my hand against my*
*master, because he is the Lord's anointed."*
—1 SAMUEL 24:10

David had several reasons to kill Saul. First, Saul had tried to kill him a few times. Second, David had been anointed as king to replace Saul because Saul rejected God. Yet David did not take revenge or even come close to it.

Revenge is God's instrument, but I justify my vengeful attempts because I use benign weapons such as gossip and exaggeration. If I get serious about revenge, I may even use sarcastic jibes or I may withdraw from the relationship.

I'm learning to lay down my weapons and try to reconcile troublesome relationships. When that doesn't work, all I can do is lay the relationship before God and say, "I have done what I can do. I surrender it to you. Fix it when the time is right."

*God, help me reconcile with others*
*instead of taking revenge.*

I can let God tend to God's business.

# *Choosing Camaraderie*

*Saul said to his armor-bearer, "Draw your sword and run me through, or these uncircumcised fellows will come and run me through and abuse me." But his armor-bearer was terrified and would not do it; so Saul took his own sword and fell on it.*
—1 SAMUEL 31:4

Suicide seems like an escape, but it is the ultimate unhealthy isolation. Isolation didn't help me with my eating disorder; suicide won't help me with life. Occasionally I find myself toying with this unhealthy thought, but I choose now to talk to someone instead. I choose camaraderie over isolation.

Camaraderie helps me because it gives me the perspective I need. In my isolation, I become like Saul, projecting the worst possible result in every situation. The more I think about it, the more hopeless I feel. The camaraderie of a telephone call or a support-group meeting, or pouring out my soul to God awakens me out of my isolated stupor and shakes me into remembering that with God there is always hope.

*Please rescue me, God, when I lose sight of the miraculous hope available in you.*

I can choose fellowship with those who understand me over self-destructive thoughts.

# *Confrontation Palpitations*

*Then Nathan said to David,
"You are the man!"*—2 SAMUEL 12:7

Not every accusation that's been made about me was true, but some have been true. When I'm confronted, I usually tell confronters that I will consider their words and get back to them. If I try to respond immediately, I either defend myself or I take all the blame. I have no objectivity until the rush of embarrassment dies down. Then I can see if it's true, and if it is, I can admit that to myself, to God, and to my confronter.

Not everyone confronts me as directly as Nathan confronted David. One friend may tell another how disgusting it is that I scarf down my food. I may be embarrassed for days because I know it's true. By the time I share it with a support group, I say, "This friend was right. I do scarf down my food. This is one more thing I need to add to my abstinence."

*God, please help me listen to those who
confront me even if it's unpleasant.*

I may learn more from friends' harsh,
confrontive words than
from their kind ones.

# Wrong? Not Me!

*Then David said to Nathan, "I have sinned against the Lord."*—2 SAMUEL 12:13

For years I couldn't admit I was wrong, and I hid my faults as David hid his affair with Bathsheba. Their deception cost Bathsheba's husband his life just as my unacknowledged faults caused my friends and family to suffer.

It may be difficult to admit I'm wrong, but it's even more difficult to keep up the facade of being right. I have to keep rationalizing my behavior and reviewing my defense. I miss out on a lot of warmth and fun because I have to keep a distance that reminds everyone that I was right. It can be exhausting.

When I admit I'm wrong as David finally did, I feel relieved. There is no shame in being human and making mistakes. There may be consequences, but God is gracious; I can always start over.

*Give me the courage and sense of security in your love to admit my faults.*

It is a sign of strength to admit
I am wrong.

# Go Where the Love Is

*You love those who hate you and hate those
who love you.*—2 SAMUEL 19:6

To prove myself I have tried to win over those who do not like me. Proving myself is important only when I think poorly of myself. I spent a lot of time impressing them and feeling bad because they prefer others over me. The craziness of my compulsive nature means that I also treated those I love poorly because I take them for granted. They don't benefit from my best behavior, but they suffer with my worst.

The saying "Go where the love is" means that I should enjoy people who like me and not worry about everyone else. I'm learning to accept that the relationships I have are enough; actually, they're plenty! If I am going to be friends with someone who currently doesn't like me, it will happen. I don't have to chase it.

*Thank you for those who like me, God.*
*Open my eyes to their needs and delights.*

God provides the relationships I need.
My job is to give to those relationships.

# *Just One Hero*

*He reached down from on high and took
hold of me; he drew me out of deep
waters.*—2 SAMUEL 22:17

Ultimately, every person on this earth will fail or disappoint me because they're only human. I've had such fears of abandonment that I've expected my parents, my sibling, my friends, and my spouse to be everything I need. When any of them disappointed me, I looked for comfort (or was it revenge?) in my overeating.

No one can truly rescue me but God. Bible passages such as today's portray God as the kind of hero out of the old West or from an exotic space adventure who draws me out of deep trouble just in the nick of time. God is the one who comes for me and helps me. He's the only one who can legitimately take that responsibility because only he is divinely equipped to do so.

*God, I look to you to be God to me.*

I can let friends be friends and God
be the one who rescues me.

# More Open Spaces

*He brought me out into a spacious place.*
—2 SAMUEL 22:20

Recovery feels like a spacious place because I can breathe deeply and relax so easily. I don't feel so tense because I'm no longer conniving to get food and work it off. I'm not so needy, and I don't have to prove anything to anyone.

My choices are no longer limited. I can pick up and go somewhere at the last minute without wondering what I'll eat, if I'll like it enough, and when I'll exercise. I'm free to gratefully eat whatever meal is put in front of me without wishing it were gooey chocolate or a gourmet diet food.

My heart and mind are more spacious, too. Listening to others share their struggles opens me to people I would have otherwise shelved. I see how wrong I've been about people and how much I have to learn.

*Help me to relax in this spacious place, God.*

I have many choices and I can enjoy them.

# Worth Rescuing

*He rescued me because he delighted*
*in me.*—2 SAMUEL 22:20

Many people put up with me; some enjoy me; others even admire me. But God is the one who delights in me.

- Yes, I make mistakes, but God delights in me.
- Yes, I'm a compulsive eater-spender-volunteer, but God still delights in me.
- Yes, I hurt people's feelings, but God keeps delighting in me.
- Yes, I fall short of my potential at times, but God continues to delight in me.
- Yes, I forget to delight in his presence, but God doesn't stop delighting in me.

I'm not a second-best kid with God, no matter what I've done or what's happened to me. I'm always first rate.

*Thank you, God, that you delight in someone*
*as flawed and broken as me.*

God not only loves me, God likes me.

# Doing My Part

*I insist on paying you for it. I will not
sacrifice to the Lord my God burnt offerings
that cost me nothing.*—2 SAMUEL 24:24

I'm asking myself less frequently, "How little can
I get by with?" The integrity and rigorous honesty
required in recovery stirs in me the desire to do my
part. Friends talk about how they refuse to do shoddy
work and how they no longer feel comfortable steal-
ing time from their employers. They want to honor
God by offering him work that costs them effort.
Their example shows me that the softer, easier, lazier
way of my culture offers only guilt and shame.

As a result, I am no longer interested in how
much I can get out of someone or how little I can
spend for a quality service. I feel cheapened by
uneven relationships in which I do more taking than
giving. I like wanting to do the best I can by others.
It feels good.

*God, please help me escape
the free-lunch mentality.*

I want to offer to God and to others
the best I can give.

# Making Decisions

*So give your servant a discerning heart to
govern your people and to distinguish
between right and wrong.*—1 KINGS 3:8

Should I tell the truth if it hurts someone? If I
try to help this person, will it increase their problems? What is a fair consequence for my child's
misbehavior?

As my recovery continues, I think more clearly.
I'm not making decisions based on how I can get my
inflated needs met or on what people will think of me
if I do certain things.

When faced with a difficult decision or judgment, that inner serenity kicks in, and I brainstorm
ideas for handling the situation. As I wait, the answers
usually come to me. These decisions used to baffle
me, but I sense that my God-given intuition is return-
ing. I'm learning to trust myself again.

*God, help me continue to sort out
my priorities and motives so I can make
wise decisions.*

As I dismantle the old negative tapes
in my head, I can get in touch with my
healthy decision-making capabilities.

# *Rest Therapy*

*"I have had enough, Lord," [Elijah] said.
"Take my life; I am no better than my
ancestors." Then he lay down under the tree
and fell asleep.*—1 KINGS 19:4–5

Because food made me feel good, I thought I was invincible. If I was sick, I got up, went to work, came home, and did routine chores. The drivenness behind the eating permeated every area of my life. I needed to prove that I was good enough, better and stronger than others.

When Elijah, a prophet of great faith, became discouraged he got away from it all. He poured his heart out to God and he took a nap. A little later, an angel awakened him and fed him and then he rested again.

It's OK for me to rest or to take a day off when I'm exhausted. Recovery is an exhausting business, and I need to take care of myself.

*Help me to take good care of myself.*

God wants me to have proper rest
and refreshment.

# *The Power of Gentleness*

*After the earthquake came fire, but the Lord was not in the fire. And after the fire came a gentle whisper.*—1 KINGS 19:12

God was not in the wind, earthquake, or fire, but he was in the gentle whisper of all things.

I want to show God's mighty gentleness to myself. I'm not the best-looking person in the world, but I'm still loved. I'm not completing this new task on time, but that's normal with new tasks.

Gentleness is a quality that I have undervalued and underestimated. It has so much power behind it. When I speak gently, my angry child gives up that venom. When I look gently at my friend, she releases the full force of her frustration, cleansing her jagged emotions. When I speak a soft phrase, my spouse sets his self-esteem back on the road to restoration.

*God, teach me to handle myself and others with the gentleness you use with me.*

A soft smile can often accomplish what a shout cannot.

# *Releasing the Secrets*

*The Israelites secretly did things against
the Lord their God that were not right.*
—2 KINGS 17:9

Eating by myself outfoxes others. No one knows
how much or how little I eat. Eating a sandwich
before meeting someone for lunch helped me look
controlled as I ordered a small salad or glass of iced
tea. People never knew about the way I pinched food
here and there, about my hourly snacks or my sweet
tooth binges. It was my secret life.

"We're as sick as our secrets," goes the saying.
Israel never faced her secrets and within a few years
she was scattered and lost in history. I need to share
my disgusting eating patterns and the lengths to which
I've gone to get junk food. I need to tell how much or
how little I've weighed and how I feel about that. In
releasing these secrets, I find relief. As my capacity to
be rigorously honest grows, so do I.

*Help me see that secrecy is what gives my
secrets their power and that when I share
them, they become harmless.*

I can share my secrets and know that
I am still loved.

# Mixed Truth

*They worshipped the Lord, but they also
served their own gods in accordance with the
customs of the nations from which they had
been brought.*—2 KINGS 17:33

It's easy to mix the truths of recovery from an
eating disorder with the popular ideas of my culture.
I need to be vigilant about this.

Recovery from an eating disorder is not dieting,
fad dieting, health-food dieting, or compulsive dieting. My abstinence will follow a healthy normal eating pattern.

Recovery requires self-examination, but I don't
put myself ahead of the rest of the world. In my effort to release my shame, I don't inflate my image
of who I am but I let it become rooted in God's opinion of me.

Recovery is not about conquering, gaining self-
control, and becoming sufficient. It's about surrendering myself to God.

The truth works. I won't compromise it.

*God, reveal to me my legalistic practices,
quick fixes, and egotistical ideas.*

I can listen to other's ideas and test
them against God's basic requirement
of me: surrender.

# *Unmasking God*

*Look to the Lord and his strength; seek his face always.*—1 CHRONICLES 16:11

Seek his face is such a mystical and religious-sounding phrase. How does someone do this?

Seek? I have let my eating disorder block out God's presence and assistance. I must reacquaint myself with him.

His face? I seek not only God, but his face. I discover who God is behind all those masks I've put on him—policeman, Santa Claus, bellhop. I find that he is the divine parent who cares so much for me that he sacrificed his own child to make things right.

Always? God cannot be absorbed in a year, ten years, or a hundred years. Seeking God is a lifetime task, but an enjoyable one!

*God, I want to seek you and quit seeing you with the masks I've placed on you.*

Even after I find God, I go on seeking him.

# *Discouraging Influences*

*Then the peoples around them set out to discourage the people of Judah and make them afraid to go on [re]building [the temple].*—EZRA 4:4

People have discouraged me from recovering from my eating disorder. Friends with whom I used to eat compulsively have made fun of my abstinence. People with whom I have been enmeshed have not liked it that I am developing my own identity and do not share every secret with them. Even some of those to whom I've made amends do not talk to me. I'm baffled at times, but I refuse to worry about them.

I pray that these people will accept my new attitudes, but I can't let their lack of acceptance distract me. I can't change others, but I can, with God's help, change myself, and that is what is happening. I have been waiting for this change all my life. I feel free to know and love God, to know and love others.

*God, please tame the tongues of those who discourage me.*

I can't change others' opinions of me, but I can refuse to give their opinions power over me.

# Sharing from the Gut

*While Ezra was praying and confessing,*
*weeping and throwing himself down before*
*the house of God, a large crowd . . . gathered*
*around him. They too wept bitterly.*
—EZRA 10:1

The difference between a humdrum support-group meeting and a boldly empowering one is rigorous honesty. When others confess and humble themselves, I feel safe enough to do the same. The power of others' honesty nearly bounces off me, empowering me to do the same. I feel safe in this kind of group because whatever I say will be accepted.

People say, "Go to that meeting—it's a good one" or "There's not much honesty at that meeting." No matter what meeting I attend, I can share my secrets and confess my sick behaviors and defects of character. I do this for myself, but the power will bounce off others as well.

*Thank you for support-group meetings, God.*
*Help me share myself as honestly as possible.*

I can use each support-group meeting
to advance my recovery.

# *Good Grieving*

*When I heard these things, I sat down and
wept. For some days I mourned and fasted
and prayed before the God of heaven.*
—NEHEMIAH 1:4

Grieving is good for me. If I had fully faced my
grief, I would not have had to use an eating disorder
to calm myself. Now I find myself grieving over past
hurts I've never faced, over my defects of character,
over catastrophic world events, over friends who were
abused as children.

If my friend tells me she's moving away, I celebrate with her if she's happy, but I cry in front of her,
too. I need to show her how I will miss her presence,
and she needs to see how much she means to me.

Grieving isn't weak. Nehemiah, a shrewd politi-
cian who worked in the court of the Persian empire,
sat in the ruins of his homeland and grieved over its
destruction. Then he went on to lead a movement to
rebuild it. That is how change begins.

*I surrender all my grief to you, Lord,
along with my need to look strong.*

I can grieve when I feel
the need to do so.

# Gathered,
# Not Scattered

*If you are unfaithful, I will scatter you among
the nations, but if you return to me and obey
my commands, then . . . I will gather them
from there and bring them to the place
I have chosen. . . .* —NEHEMIAH 1:8–9

Scattered thoughts and feelings have preceded
my episodes with my eating disorder. I feel aimless,
and I want so many things that I want nothing. My
drivenness has forced me to choose my most urgent
need: to overeat, diet, purge, or starve.

*Scattering* has been a curse on nations throughout history, and I can see why. I feel miserable when
I'm scattered inside. *Gathering* again healed a nation's
curse, and my recovery allows God to gather me
again. Being gathered helps me focus on specific purposes and push away my drivenness to eat, diet, look
good, or succeed. I experience some of my most content moments when I gather myself before God. I center myself on him, and we both know I am headed for
health and wholeness in Him.

*Gather together the scattered parts of me,
and draw me to yourself, God.*

The feeling of scatteredness can leave me.

# Facing Authority Figures

*I was very much afraid, but I said to the king, ". . . why should my face not look sad when the city where my fathers are buried lies in ruins? . . ."*—NEHEMIAH 2:2–3

Power struggles with authority figures or having to appease them create inner turmoil, which lures me into thoughts of food. When there's a great stone face on a supervisor at work, a committee chairperson, or the manager of a store in which I wish to return an item, I feel there is no way to get through to them. So I react by either coming on too strong or becoming a wimp, then munching out or starving.

No more. Since I've tried to quit blaming, complaining, and people pleasing, I can now listen to their concerns, state my concerns, and negotiate. Even if nothing works, I have the satisfaction of knowing I'm behaving like a problem solver. I no longer let these situations ruin my life by responding with compulsive behavior.

*God, please give me understanding, tact, and creativity to deal with each authority figure in my life.*

I can respond to authority figures without getting upset.

# *Farewell, Rescuer*

*I had not told anyone what my God had put
in my heart to do for Jerusalem. . . . By night
I went out . . . examining the walls of
Jerusalem, which had been broken
down. . . .* —NEHEMIAH 2:11–13

News flash: I don't have to rescue the world. Now when I think God is putting something in my heart to do, I try to make sure it's from God and not my egotistical need to rescue. Now I don't rush in so quickly. I wait and pray and try to determine what God wants me to do. Like Nehemiah poking around in the night, I investigate first. I may not even tell anyone what I'm up to. Or I may run the idea past someone who understands the situation better.

The results of this cautious but God-driven approach are astounding. I don't burn out. I give my whole heart to something with no regret. I don't expect results or gratefulness, because I'm doing it for God, not for anyone else. He supplies the energy, results, and solutions.

*Please show me the ways you want me to
serve you, God, and how to approach them.*

I can carefully choose the ways I will serve
God passionately.

# Is There Rubble in My Abstinence?

*Meanwhile the people in Judah said, "The strength of the laborers is giving out and there is so much rubble that we cannot rebuild the wall."*—NEHEMIAH 4:10

Some seemingly innocent behaviors, which I once thought were allowable for my abstinence, become rubble. They put me in slippery situations that call for such strength that I lose or barely maintain my abstinence. Usually I am more deeply attached to these behaviors than I would like to admit. Can I keep potato chips in my house without binging on them? Am I drinking too many diet sodas? Am I overexercising? Are my meal portions larger or smaller than they need to be?

These are the tough questions I must ask myself about my abstinence in order to clear away the rubble. Only as I do that can I rebuild my habits with food from the inside out.

*Help me surrender my rubble behaviors so I can pursue my recovery in a healthier way.*

I can clear away rubble behaviors, even if it doesn't make sense to others.

# Justice in All My Dealings

*So I continued, "What you are doing is not right. . . . Give back to them immediately their fields, vineyards, olive groves, and houses."*—NEHEMIAH 5:9, 11

In the past I was honest—when a sales clerk gave me incorrect extra change, I gave it back. But I was dishonest in other ways. I blamed others for my problems and made excuses for my weight difficulties.

Because I wasn't rigorously honest, I didn't insist that others deal with me in just ways. I knew I wasn't playing it exactly straight, so why should they have to?

Now that I'm working on becoming rigorously honest, I'm less afraid to ask people who intimidate me or people I love if things are fair. I'm not policing others' morals, but I'm also not afraid to stand up for myself in a candid, polite way. Honesty is no longer such a scary thing to me.

*God, help me deal truthfully with others and ask them to do the same with me.*

Being honest about myself makes me less afraid to ask others to be honest.

# *Apologies Don't Go On Forever*

*All the people had been weeping as they
listened to the words of the Law. Nehemiah
said, ". . . do not grieve, for the joy of the
Lord is your strength."*—NEHEMIAH 8:9–10

I have cried over the way I've dealt with myself,
my friends, and my family in the past. In my drivenness, I have ignored them and judged them without
mercy. Once I've surrendered and made amends, it's
time to surrender my guilt, too. Apologizing over and
over doesn't help; it makes everyone feel worse.

It's time for restoration. I can celebrate and be
happy. God is showing me my defects of character,
and he will change me if I keep surrendering them to
him. It's time to be grateful for what God is doing in
my life. This leads me to surrender more of myself
to God.

*You are my strength, and I am glad that
I have surrendered to you.*

Restoration is better than regret.

# *Fear of Success?*

*Esther was lovely in form and features. . . .
Now the king was attracted to Esther more
than to any of the other women. . . . So he
set a royal crown on her head and made
her queen. . . .*—ESTHER 2:7, 17

What terrible things will happen to me if I look
attractive? Will I be swept away by a tyrant who
drinks too much? That's what happened to the young
Jewish girl, Esther. With God's strength, she confronted this tyrant-king when it meant saving her
people even though she feared for her life.

I won't face a tyrant-king, but I have challenges
of my own: Can I be comfortable with myself at a normal weight? Can I handle situations I haven't had to
face before?

I can do these things if I surrender each scary
feeling and situation to God. I can do them if I continue to rely on the strength of others like me who
have eating disorders. I can do them if I get excited
about God's purposes for me instead of being obsessed with my fears.

*I surrender my fears to you, and I ask you
to use me in dynamic ways for your causes.*

I don't have to be afraid of weighing
an average weight.

# *Feel Pretty?*
# *Pretty Awful!*

*. . . she had to complete twelve months of
beauty treatments prescribed for the women,
six months with oil of myrrh and six with
perfumes and cosmetics.*—ESTHER 2:12

Is it OK for me to try to look attractive? Is it a
worthwhile effort to do what I can with what I have?

Some of Esther's girlfriends must have clucked
their tongues about the excessiveness of twelve
months of beauty treatments. But Esther followed
this beauty pageant regimen because her mentor-
cousin advised her to do so. It turned out to be God's
will, and Esther saved her people.

What is God's will for my appearance? It isn't
overattention to it as it was for Esther, but it doesn't
mean neglecting myself or looking dowdy either. I am
growing more comfortable with the appearance that
God gave me, and I pay attention to it without over-
doing it. I enjoy making myself as easy on the other
person's eyes as possible.

*I surrender my appearance to you, God,
and I ask you to help me cultivate a healthy
attitude about it.*

God will not abandon me if I maintain
a proper weight and have fun trying
to look attractive.

# *Expectations of God*

> At this, Job got up and tore his robe . . .
> and said: ". . . the Lord gave and
> the Lord has taken away. May the name
> of the Lord be praised." In all this, Job did
> not sin by charging God with wrongdoing.
> —JOB 1:20–22

When crises occur in my life, I realize that I expected certain things of God such as decent food, clothing, and shelter; a family that loves me and doesn't get into trouble; a job I like; neighbors that don't play loud music all night; minor sicknesses only; eighty years of life. When these expectations are not fulfilled, I become bitter. In the past I took care of this bitterness with my eating disorder.

As I hear the stories of others with eating disorders and as I attempt abstinence, I become more grateful and humble. This affects my relationship with God so that I'm less likely to make demands on him and charge him with wrongdoing. I'm more likely to surrender my expectations of God to God and accept and endure problems.

*I come to you, God, with gratefulness for*
*what you have given me in this life.*

I can stop expecting things from God and
become grateful for what I have.

# DAY 82

## *Wordless Comfort*

*Then they sat down on the ground with him
for seven days and seven nights. No one said
a word to him, because they saw how great
his suffering was.* —JOB 2:13

When Job lost his children and livestock, his
friends came to him and sat in silence with him for
the first seven days.

In the past, I frequently offered what I thought
were eloquent words of comfort. But in support
groups I watch what happens without my eloquent
answers ever being vocalized. People find comfort by
talking through problems without interruption, by
crying without interruption, and by hearing God's
promptings themselves.

Perhaps this is what is meant by the term *ministry of presence*. The best comfort I can offer is being
with others in their hurt. I can simply say to a grieving person, "Can I sit beside you for a while?" or "Do
you want to talk?"

*Thank you, God, for your empowering
presence in my life. Help me communicate
that presence to others in grief.*

I can surrender my need
to appear eloquent.

# Powerlessness Empowers

*Do I have any power to help myself, now
that success has been driven from me?*
—JOB 6:13

Power is supposedly linked with success, and powerlessness is linked with failure. Powerless people have little to say in politics, economics, or even relationships.

By surrendering my eating disorder, I'm agreeing to do an unbelievable thing: to give up power. I admit that I am powerless over my eating disorder.

This works because it melts my drivenness to overpower my problems. This drivenness backfired on me and sabotaged success instead of creating it. As I give up my attempts to be powerful, I am free to invite the greatest power of all to take over and to do for me what I cannot do for myself. This is real power.

*I surrender to your great power, God, and I
give up my driven attempts to control my life.*

I admit that I am powerless over
my eating disorder.

# To Feel Bad Is to Be Human

*I will speak out in the anguish of my spirit,*
*I will complain in the bitterness of my soul.*
—JOB 7:11

I desperately wanted to stop feeling bad, sad, and mad. I've overeaten and starved to get rid of those feelings, but this only buried them. My feelings became bitter in the depths of my soul, and they ended up paralyzing me emotionally.

I'm learning that feeling bad is part of being human. As long I live on earth, it's going to be this way, and there is no easy escape from bad feelings. I make decisions about how I will live this prone-to-trouble existence.

I have decided to go through these bad feelings abstinent. This means I will experience them in their full severity and I can use tools to process them: journaling, praying, calling friends, and going to support groups. No matter what, I will not resort to my eating disorder.

*God, give me the strength to survive my*
*intense feelings and remain abstinent.*

I can now work through bad feelings
because I have the courage, the tools, and
the repaired relationship with God.

# When I Least Expect It

*[God] performs wonders that cannot be
fathomed, miracles that cannot be
counted.*—JOB 9:10

I am learning that I don't have life figured out.
When I am sure someone is headed for trouble, they
turn around. Just when I've projected that the road
ahead will be rough, it isn't. God keeps intervening
when I least expect him to do so.

I don't predict the future anymore. God has a
thousand unknowns I don't know about. What I
think is the worst possible situation may turn out
to be the best thing that has happened to me. I'm less
sure of myself, but more sure of God. I'm less sure
of exactly how I'll cope, but more sure that I eventually will.

*God, help me enjoy the ways
you work unexpectedly.*

The door is always open for God
to do the unexpected.

# Put On a Happy Face?

*If I say, "I will forget my complaint, I will change my expression, and smile," I still dread all my sufferings. . . .* —JOB 9:27

People often ask me how I could have been so miserable in my eating disorder, but seemed so happy. That's easy. I faked it. I denied that my inner pain existed except when relationships forced me to face it.

I was good at looking good, looking happy, and looking fine. Like Job, I could forget my complaint and smile but still dread my inner suffering. My eating disorder facilitated this pseudo-happiness because it numbed my pain.

Now I tell people how I'm really feeling: I'm OK, I'm stressed, I'm "hangin' in there." I feel free to be liked or disliked for who I am, not who I pretend to be. It's important to admit that I don't feel wonderful all the time, so I don't encourage others to put on a false happy face either.

*God, help me become a genuine, authentic person.*

I give up the dishonest image of being perpetually fine.

# *Lifting up My Head*

*Then you will lift up your face without
shame; you will stand firm and without
fear.*—JOB 11:15

The shame of my eating disorder made me silent
about my true self. I felt a desperation so quiet that I
seemed to do less than exist. I was less than nothing.
I hung my head and looked away when people, especially healthy people, looked at me.

By surrendering my eating disorder to God, I'm
allowing him to lift the shame from me. As I reach out
toward him, I find that I'm standing, even standing
firm. I'm not afraid, but I'm confident.

All this happens because I accept that God values me no matter what I do or have done. He loves me
beyond anything I can imagine.

*Help me understand, God, that you have
rescued me from shame's power.*

As I admit my powerlessness
and surrender to God,
I am freed of shame.

# *How Much Advice*
# *Is Enough?*

*To God belong wisdom and power; counsel
and understanding are his.*—JOB 12:13

Contemporary culture turns people into advice
junkies. While I should seek the counsel of advisers
(Prov. 15:22), I can also overdo it. It is as if I pull up
to a filling station and say, "I'll take three how-tos and
two formulas."

Counsel is helpful, but at times I lean too heavily
on others and I don't seek God's counsel. With all
this chitchat, it is easy to talk about problems but do
little about them.

For now I can play catch-up with the advice I've
been given. I can bring it before God and let him help
me figure out how to follow it.

*God, help me consider other's advice but
to do what I think you are leading me to do.*

It is my responsibility to weigh advice
and follow through as I see fit.

# *Hitting Bottom*

*Though he slay me, yet will
I hope in him.*—JOB 13:15

In times of crises, I have toyed with the thought of giving up on God and forgetting that I ever believed in him. Yet when I'm at my worst, I need God the most.

When I turn to God in crises, I change. I'm more pliable. So if he speaks to me about my compulsive behavior or defects of character, I'm more likely to surrender them because I have nothing to lose.

There is never a good time or place to give up on God. Even in good times, I realize that he is really all I have, and actually, all I need to survive.

*God, help me see that I never have to give
up on you.*

No matter how cornered I feel,
God can sustain me.

# Opinions Anyone?

*Would [a wise man] argue with useless*
*words, with speeches that have no value?*
—JOB 15:3

Winning and being right used to mean everything to me. For days afterward, I would dwell on what I should have said to win an argument. What was at stake all those times? Usually, my flagging self-esteem.

My opinions have become less important because I don't have to prove myself anymore. I'm filling that inner vacuum with the assurance that God loves me, with the camaraderie of other strugglers like me, and with the relief that I'm not a terrible person after all.

I may still hold controversial opinions, but I don't have to bless others with them whenever they ask. And when I do give opinions, I can abandon my attorneylike attitudes and leave my hearers free to think whatever they like.

*God, I let go of my neediness*
*to be heard. Help me present my opinions*
*in a congenial way.*

I don't have to take my opinions
so seriously.

# *Mad at God?*

*Why has your heart carried you away, and why do your eyes flash, so that you vent your rage against God . . . ?*—JOB 15:12–13

I, too, have raged against God. I've screamed and yelled. Or, I've vented my anger in more subtle ways by griping about the church or muttering flip, cynical one-liners to God. Or I've raged against him while gorging my body with food or starving it.

I'm learning to ventilate these angry feelings to God in a different way. I write it out in journals, talk it out in support groups, and pray it out (sometimes rather loudly) in private places. Then after I ventilate, I express my hope and faith that he will do something to rescue me from my anger. I'm beginning to trust that he loves me even when I'm angry, so I tell him that I trust him with as much faith as I can muster.

*God, I want to trust you with every detail of my life, even when I'm angry about those details!*

I can talk things out with God and reconcile with him.

# *Enjoying God*

*Surely then you will find delight in the
Almighty and will lift up your face to
God.*—JOB 22:26

The idea of finding delight in God sounds a little
odd. I've loved God as a child loves a parent, but I can
actually enjoy him, too.

Recovery helps me do this. Because I no longer
**judge** myself so harshly, I don't assume that he's judging me harshly, too. I experience his grace and mercy
from other compulsive eaters like myself who have
loved me in spite of the sickest of my behaviors. I see
that God loves me in the same way, and I feel accepted by him.

I'm learning that God is surprising and interesting. I see all the unexpected, meaningful things that
happen to me as gifts from him. So I thank him for all
the attention he pays to me.

*God, I like the idea of enjoying being
with you. Help me to explore that.*

It is possible to enjoy God's presence.

# DAY 93

# *Wisdom for Compulsives*

*But where can wisdom be found? Where does understanding dwell?*—JOB 28:12

I have given up on my old sources of wisdom such as diet cookbooks, dieting books, and exercise manuals. This wisdom did not solve my problems. Neither did the wisdom of friends who told me how to purge or who explained why it was so great to starve.

These sources of wisdom may work for others who aren't compulsive, but they don't work for me. I am driven. Repairs aren't enough.

Even after I declare that I've completely over-hauled my attitude, that old mind-set calls out in the form of new dieting fads, liquid diets, and exercise gadgets. Once again, I can choose not to make these things part of my abstinence. Recovery means surrendering my drives to God daily and banding with others like myself. This works, and this I will do.

*God, help me to recognize when I'm leaning on my old sources of wisdom, and help me turn to you.*

My old dieting wisdom doesn't work.
I surrender it.

# *Learn by Doing*

*. . . to shun evil is understanding.*
—JOB 28:28

It is a normal feeling to want to understand abstinence before jumping into it. But I ask, How can abstinence work if it's not a diet? (Less food is ingested, so a normal weight *slowly* returns.) Why is an eating disorder a spiritual issue? (Because it defines who I am, which is a spiritual issue.) Still, these answers may not make sense to me.

Thankfully, I can quit analyzing and just try abstinence. As I progress, I make mistakes and discover things for myself. I may hear an insight I've heard many times, but it finally makes sense to me. As I do the footwork, I understand more.

Abstinence and wholeness can only be understood by *doing*—shunning my compulsive ways and seeking God. They cannot be understood unless I put them into practice.

*God, help me shun my former practices so*
*I may understand life better.*

Recovery is a learn-as-you-grow activity.

# A Symbol of Hope

*When I smiled at them, they scarcely*
*believed it; the light of my face was precious*
*to them.*—JOB 29:24

As my eating disorder became worse, hope drained out of my life until I forgot what hope felt like. I wanted hope, but it was so intangible, so elusive, so feeling-oriented. I had trouble being hopeful.

The smile of recovering friends has become a symbol of hope. I see a rush of joy on their faces as they see me come into the room. We laugh so hard we cry as we share our sick and silly behaviors. We smile until our faces glow with joy and pride for each other as we share our progress. I see more honest smiles than I've seen for a long time. Slowly, my hope returns.

*God, thank you for the smiles of others*
*and the hope they can offer me.*

I can offer my smile and a lit-up face
as a symbol of hope to others.

# Living in My Feelings

*Terrors overwhelm me; my dignity is driven away as by the wind, my safety vanishes like a cloud.*—JOB 30:15

Turning my back on food means that I feel my emotions in their full intensity. Some days it seems as if I'm living in my feelings, and they chase all logic out the back door of my mind. Then I am left alone with those negative feelings and they threaten to thrash me. As one recovering compulsive overeater put it, "My head is like a dangerous neighborhood. I'm afraid to go in there without someone else."

I'm learning to take others with me into that dangerous neighborhood of my mind. I call friends and share my feelings, thus exposing my feelings to reality. I journal about those feelings and sort out which ones are true. Facing that truth helps me welcome my logic back into my head, which can be a calming influence on my feelings.

*Thank you for giving me feelings, but help me to process them in a healthy way.*

Feelings can help me, but I need to keep them in touch with reality.

# More Will Be Revealed

*If I have concealed my sin as men do, by
hiding my guilt in my heart because I so
feared the crowd. . . .*—JOB 31:33

I have concealed some of my sin so well that I
don't even know what it is. I think I've forgiven people when I haven't. I think I've been generous when
I haven't.

God reveals more to me as I surrender more of
myself. As he sees that I am ready, he shows me how
I've wounded a person's heart, how I've obsessed on
money, and how I've ignored difficult people.

I can accept these things better as I quit beating
myself up so much. As I shower grace on myself, he
is free to show me what I am often like and to give me
his overflowing, healing grace.

*I yield myself to you, God, to show me
how I need to grow.*

I'm not the person I used to be,
and I'm not the person
God is helping me become.

# *Self-Obsession*

*But Elihu ... became very angry with Job for justifying himself rather than God.*—JOB 32:2

Job's accusers tried to find something wrong with Job, but could fault him for only one thing: He justified himself rather than God. I justify myself to the point that I am obsessed with myself.

When accused, I defend myself with elaborate reasons. I have a high-toned excuse for each of my faults. I have crafty ways of designing conversations that make me look good and subtle ways of praising my own efforts. I constantly ask myself, "Is anyone looking at me?" "Did I say the right thing?" "Am I getting as much done as I should?" "Am I truly happy?" "Will I ever make it in life?"

Recovering from my eating disorder helps me address my inner issues, but it also frees me from the need to focus on myself. That helps me reach out to others, which in turn, frees me from being hung up on myself.

*God, help me catch myself in my moments of habitual self-obsession and turn my thoughts outward.*

I can be genuinely interested
in others when I quit being preoccupied
with myself.

# *Breaking the Isolation*

*I must speak and find relief; I must open my
lips and reply.*—JOB 32:20

Talking to people who also struggle with an eating disorder is important because I've spent so much time in isolation that I've developed some dark behaviors that need to come out to the light. Finally, I can speak the unspeakable about my past experiences, my eating disorder, and my darkest feelings.

Yet I want to be careful not to "get sick" on others by speaking in personal conversations so honestly that it's difficult for them to tolerate. It's easy to confuse other small groups with support groups in which nearly anything is appropriate, but I'm learning to distinguish appropriate settings from inappropriate ones.

In appropriate settings, the relief comes because there are others like me who make me feel loved and accepted—finally.

*God, help me share things that
will help me recover.*

I can and should share freely
in appropriate settings.

# Listening for God to Speak

*For God does speak—now one way, now another—though many may not perceive it.*
—JOB 33:14

The voices of my compulsion are fading: Make yourself better by . . . ; Fix that person by . . . ; Stay in control by. . . . As they fade, I hear God speak more clearly.

God speaks to me through Scripture. He speaks through books and magazines that apply scriptural principles. He speaks through people in my support group. Sometimes he speaks through the nonsense, comfort, and confrontation of my friends. He speaks through sermons—especially the ones that I think I don't need. He can even speak through the beauty of my surroundings and the patches of dying grass.

I try to listen.

*Thank you for the varied ways you guide me, God.*

I can listen for God's unlikely ways of speaking to me.

# Second-Guessing God

*How great is God—beyond our
understanding!*—JOB 36:26

With my overanalytical, private-detective mentality, I trust only what I understand. I've tried to figure out God in so many ways, but rarely does anything that happens to me make sense. Every time I second-guess what he's up to, I'm wrong. He has given me things I don't think I want and withheld things I have begged for. This used to ignite a steady burning bitterness in me and fuel my eating disorder.

I've decided to stop trying to understand God. This means that I quit peering over his shoulder to try to read the control panel. I sit back, shut my eyes, and try to enjoy the ride.

Why did I wait so long to do this?

*God, I surrender to you my need to
understand everything that happens to me.*

I don't have to understand the journey,
I just have to continue it.

# *Sleepless Anger*

*In your anger do not sin; when you are
on your beds, search your hearts
and be silent.*—PSALM 4:4

Some of my struggles do not surface during the
day. I used to wake up at night and lie in bed letting
anger and resentment take hold of me and thrash me
around for hours as I tossed and turned. I rehearsed
why I wasn't at fault and what I could have said to so-
and-so. I lost a lot of sleep.

Now I recognize this as buried anger that needs
to be faced. I can search my heart and discover what
defects of character are in operation. Then I surrender them one by one. Out of these broken moments often comes a fierce determination to do what
I can about myself and a peace to leave everyone
else alone.

*Help me work through the anger
that keeps me awake.*

The thoughts that are hidden to me in
daylight become apparent in the silence
of night.

# *Daily Abstinence*

*In the morning, O Lord, you hear my voice;*
*in the morning I lay my requests before you*
*and wait in expectation.*—PSALM 5:3

Abstinence doesn't work if I meander through life facing meals and snacktimes as they come. As I first awaken in the morning, I invite God into my life that day. Before I sit up and my feet grope for my shoes, I ask God to give me one more day of abstinence. Before breakfast, I look at my menu for the day and commit myself to what I will and won't eat that day. A party tonight? Tough; I'll enjoy the people at the party instead of the goodies.

Throughout the day, I use my tools and enjoy this new tendency to let go of the food, the anger, and the fear I needed so badly. At night, I thank God for one more day of abstinence.

Is this a dry ritual for me? No, these are moments of grace and even excitement between God and me.

*God, please help me continue using*
*this tool of abstinence.*

I commit my abstinence to God every day,
one day at a time.

# *Achievement Hunger*

*How long must I wrestle with my thoughts
and every day have sorrow in my heart?
How long will my enemy triumph over
me?*—PSALM 13:2

When will my eating disorder evaporate? When will I be recovered? I don't like the answer: Recovery is a lifelong process. That high-achieving part of myself—perhaps even the perfectionistic part—wants to get this job done, so I can move on to other things. Yet when I least expect it, the drivenness becomes strong and I would travel land and sea for a chocolate chip cookie—now!

The battle continues, but so does my progress. I keep practicing the tools of praying, calling friends, and staying abstinent one more day. Progress is not measured by my achievements, but in the way I keep turning it over to God again and again.

*I give up my need to "lick this thing" and
offer you the pieces of the puzzle, God.*

I feed my self-esteem with God's
acceptance of me, not my ability
to conquer my eating disorder.

# Practicing God's Presence

*I have set the Lord always before me.*
*Because he is at my right hand, I will*
*not be shaken.*—PSALM 16:8

Before I begin each event of my day, I invite God
to take part in it with me. I understand that God is
present everywhere, but I go through this formality
because I am learning to practice the presence of
God, to maintain conscious contact with him.

I want to be more aware of God's presence, not
so he can be a watchdog on my abstinence, but
because I'm getting to know him better. I know that
God is the person who loves me no matter what.
With my still-flagging self-esteem, I can't seem to get
enough of this unconditional acceptance.

I also practice God's presence because it gives
me a window to serenity. It helps me see more
quickly that nothing needs to rattle me into panicking, binging, or negative thinking.

*Thank you that you are always with me,*
*God; help me to desire a greater awareness*
*of your presence.*

I flourish in God's presence as if
I were a plant and God were the sun.

# *Pursuing My Dreams*

*May he give you the desire of your heart and make all your plans succeed.*—PSALM 20:4

I've pulled back from pursuing my dreams because I haven't believed in myself and I didn't think that God believed in me either. I didn't see myself as a capable person.

Now I'm learning that God has all kinds of interesting purposes for me and that he is working in me. I don't have to be shy, lazy, or withdrawn; he supplies me with the motivation and initiative I lack. I used to think I was useless, but I am not. Now, as a broken vessel for God, I am even more useful because I'm surrendering my will and I'm listening for God's direction. I am giving him my dreams, too, and asking him to show me if they are his will after all. Sometimes I don't sense his direction until I get out there and give it a try. Then I watch him open or shut doors, and his direction becomes clear to me.

*God, help me know your will about my dreams for the future.*

Since God believes in me enough to use me, I can pursue my dreams and see what happens.

# *Fear of Abandonment*

*Do not be far from me, for trouble is near
and there is no one to help.*—PSALM 22:11

One of my greatest fears is that I will be abandoned. I have been afraid that a time will come when there will be no one to help me. It may happen because I alienate so many people or because I'm not interesting enough to love. Will I survive? Will I be alone in this world?

I see now that this fear of abandonment has tainted my actions. It has made me a people pleaser —so concerned about doing and being for others that I have no idea of what I'm really like and what I want.

As I'm learning who I am to God and sense my purpose here on earth, I feel more secure. That carries me through moments in which it seems that no one comes to help.

*God, help me surrender my great fear
of abandonment to you.*

Abandonment itself can be endured;
the fear of it makes me live in panic.

# *Me and My Enemy*

*You prepare a table before me in the presence
of my enemies. You anoint my head with oil;
my cup overflows.*—PSALM 23:5

This familiar verse pictures me seated with people who don't like me yet I'm being honored with an anointing of God right in front of them! How different this picture is from the moments I've been shamed in front of others.

The spiritual enemy of God must be angry to see that I'm facing my eating disorder. He is seated at the table, and he is frustrated that I refuse to wallow in negative thinking, that I actually try to solve problems without eating, and that I find life beyond food.

When I picture this scene I can see that I belong on the side of the table opposite the spiritual enemy behind my eating disorder. I am detached from it. I now have a new separate identity.

*God, thank you for blessing me in the
presence of my spiritual enemy.*

Recovery from an eating disorder means
the clash of powerful forces.

# *Traps from the Past*

*My eyes are ever on the Lord, for only he will release my feet from the snare.*—PSALM 25:15

I would like to overlook the snares that entice me such as snacking while I fix meals, overdosing on diet drinks, and resorting to liquid diets. As God shows me that these behaviors are part of my eating disorder, they must go. My refusal to part with them tells me that I am still holding out.

Yet my goal is to completely dethrone compulsive overeating and dieting. I don't want those small behaviors to haunt me or remind me of my former great devotion to my eating disorder. If I let them, they can beat and bludgeon me and convince me I have made no progress. These former behaviors must go.

*Please give me the determination to fully surrender every part of my eating disorder to you, God.*

I can be willing, if not yet able,
to surrender the smallest of my
compulsive tendencies.

# *Brokenness Counts*

*The Lord is close to the brokenhearted and
saves those who are crushed in spirit.*
—PSALM 34:18

As long as I was self-assured and carefully re-
strained, I wasn't open to God. Now that I am desperate, broken, and crushed, I am eager for God to work
in me.

The more I admit my neediness, the more needy
I realize I am. The more I admit my faults, the less I'm
surprised by them. The more I realize how crushed
my spirit is, the more I find I'm useful to God.

My brokenness affects my body; many parts of
it don't function well. My will seems almost gone
because it was my willfulness that kept me impris-
oned. And my spirit is submitted to new disciplines
of meditation and solitude.

Yet brokenness brings me to empowerment. I
couldn't be empowered until I let go of the controls
and gave them to God.

*God, I surrender more and more
of those crushed places to you.*

Brokenness brings empowerment,
not shame.

# My Friend's Betrayal

*Even my close friend, whom I trusted, he who
shared my bread, has lifted up his heel
against me.*—PSALM 41:9

My "close friend" not only shared my bread with
me—my close friend *was* bread. It lifted its heel
against me just as I trusted it to soothe my problems
and give me confidence. Instead it hid my problems
in shadows and shriveled my confidence.

I tried to limit the drivenness of this friend, but
diets stopped working. Starving was too scary an
option. There was no talking sanity to this friend.

I am giving up bread as a close friend. I see the
inappropriateness of trusting it when I can find safe
people to trust. I can trust God as I learn to make conscious contact with him. As he changes me, I can
even trust myself. I no longer feel the sting of bread's
betrayal.

*Please flood into my life, God,
and walk and talk with me so I won't miss
my close friend so much.*

Dethroning my eating behavior as a close
friend leaves room for friendships with
God and healthy people.

# *God Honors Tears*

*Record my lament; list my tears on your
scroll—are they not in your record?*
—PSALM 56:8

In my anger, I've accused God of not caring that I'm hurting; but I know this is wrong. My tears are important to him; he honors them by recording each one. I know that I am loved and cared for.

Because I know this, I can cry without shame in front of my sponsor and support group. They honor my tears as God does. They understand that I must first grieve over my behavior before it can be changed.

Crying those tears of rigorous honesty cleanses me and releases me to make wise decisions.

*Thank you for regarding my tears with
respect, God. Help me respect them, too.*

Tears of rigorous honesty deserve respect.

# *Resting in God*

*My soul finds rest in God alone; my salvation comes from him.*—PSALM 62:1

It's a new thought to *rest* in God. I thought God wanted me to work all the time and avoid fun and relaxation. I'm learning that God doesn't say that; my depleted self-esteem tells me to feel better about myself by working all the time.

I learn to rest in God as I quit hurrying through my day to do, do, do. I stop, listen, and enjoy others. I take walks and enjoy the beauty around me. I serve because I hear a gentle nudge from God, not because no one else will do it. I don't have to please anyone but God, and when I do, others will be more pleased in the long run.

*God, plant your rest in my heart
and let it color my face and mannerisms.*

If I learn how to *be* with God,
I will eventually *do* what it is I am
supposed to do.

# Unanswered Prayers

*Praise be to God, who has not rejected my*
*prayer or withheld his love from me!*
—PSALM 66:20

I have prayed many frantic and well-thought-out prayers that don't seem to have been answered. In those moments, I felt rejected and unloved, which reinforced my suspicion that God was asleep or he didn't like me or I wasn't good enough.

As I set aside my I-want-it-now attitudes, I see that not having an immediate answer to my prayer doesn't mean that God has rejected me. He may answer my prayer with a "yes" or a "no" or a "wait." The answer is "yes" only if this is the right thing for me at exactly the right time.

I am no longer so afraid that God is rejecting me. Even when I suspect that he has not heard my prayer, I know that he has.

*Help me to trust you, God, to answer*
*my prayers for my ultimate benefit.*

Unanswered prayer is simply an answer
I don't yet understand.

# *Becoming Whole*

*You have set our iniquities before you, our
secret sins in the light of your presence.*
—PSALM 90:8

I used to pretend my eating disorder didn't exist
because I hid it so well and no one said anything
about it. When I began to feel troubled in the midst
of acting like a terribly nice person, I felt needy for
my eating disorder. It was as if I would say, "Excuse
me for a moment, God. I'll be right back. I have to do
something."

Common sense tells me to keep hiding my
secret sins, but I'm learning that it works better to
pour out my feelings to God immediately. With that
honesty, I no longer feel like two different people living in two different worlds. These two worlds have
met each other, and I am facing myself and learning
to live with myself. I am one person who isn't terribly
nice, but who also isn't so disordered. I'm simply
recovering.

*Thank you that you love me, God, even
though you see my agitated side so clearly.*

Admitting that I have an eating disorder
releases me from wearing
two different masks.

# *Protected in My Shelter*

*"He who dwells in the shelter of the Most High will rest in the shadow of the Almighty."*—PSALM 91:1

I no longer need to protect myself by withdrawing or lashing out in anger. I don't even need the protection of overeating, purging, or starving. I have found protection by renewing my God-given choices and boundaries.

I can choose to forgive instead of feeling hurt by others' comments. I can choose to overlook others' faults instead of magnifying them. I can choose to calmly speak up to those who violate my boundaries of time, privacy, or familiarity instead of resenting those people.

Healthy choices and boundaries are part of the God-given shelter that I am born with, and I will reclaim them as best I can.

*Show me, God, healthy boundaries and help me to live within them.*

No one will respect my boundaries unless I respect them myself.

# Unfathomable Forgiveness

*Praise the Lord, . . . who forgives all your sins and heals all your diseases.*—PSALM 103:1, 3

If God forgives me, then I can forgive me. God chooses to forget my past eating misbehaviors and the destructive things I've said about and felt toward people, and I need to do the same thing. Beating myself up doesn't make me a better person; it makes me a bitter person.

This overflowing forgiveness is empowering. It means that I can make amends to someone with no fear of how they will react. It means that I can stand up before others with confidence—not because I want to impress them, but because God has forgiven me. It means that I have no illusions about how wonderful I am, but that I rest in the thought that I am dearly loved by God. It means that when I fail, I can start over.

*God, help me rest in your forgiveness.*

God is more merciful to me than
I can ever be.

# How Much Is Enough?

*These all look to you to give them their food
at the proper time . . . when you open your
hand, they are satisfied with good things.*
—PSALM 104:27–28

As I start my abstinence, I ask God to show me how much food is enough to sustain me properly. When I sit down at the table, that amount may seem like too little or too much, but I can trust that God is opening his hand to me. I trust that this amount will satisfy me physically even if it doesn't satisfy my emotional needs. I now have other ways to satisfy my emotional needs—relationships, journaling, and prayer.

I, who have not trusted others well, am taking a big step by committing my food to God. It toughens and strengthens my relationship with him as I ask, "Are you sure about this, God?" Then I walk in that trust.

*My daily food is a sacred gift from you,
and I value your judgments.*

I can trust God, the blesser himself,
to distribute his blessings well.

# *Switching Snares*

*They worshiped their idols, which became a snare to them.*—PSALM 106:36

As an admitted worshiper of food and thinness, I'm a prime candidate to worship something else as I become abstinent from my eating disorder. New obsessions appear in front of me as silvery idols to snare me. I may become overly preoccupied with my newly discovered sexuality; fun and entertainment; work and productivity; even self-improvement.

I can surrender each idol and turn it over to God. If I don't, an innocent substance can become a snare for me because of my inner neediness. I must, once again, let God do for me what I cannot do for myself.

*God, help me see these silvery idols as the traps they really are, and surrender them.*

Whatever I spend too much time thinking about is my idol.

# *Unlimited Love*

*Let them give thanks to the Lord for his*
*unfailing love and his wonderful deeds for*
*men.*—PSALM 107:21

No matter how I look or how negatively my body compares to magazine ads, God loves me. No matter how I feel—angry, frustrated, or withdrawn—God loves me.

I can trust God not to think less of me because I'm not improving fast enough. He is the one who will not desert me when I blow my abstinence. He is the one who will scoop me up out of my heap of exhaustion and help me walk again.

God's love will never fail me. I can't do anything to make him stop loving me.

*Thank you that you never reject me, ignore*
*me, or harshly scold me, God.*

God's love is not limited by my flaws.

# Digesting Scripture

*I meditate on your precepts and consider
your ways.*—PSALM 119:15

Some days I gobble down Scripture verses about
as fast as I used to eat M & Ms. I feel no enjoyment,
just the need to get through the bag—or the Bible
passage.

The idea of savoring Scripture is new. I can read
a few verses, shut my eyes to block out distractions,
and consider what these verses mean in my life. If
God were going to speak to me through this passage,
what would he say?

I can't say for sure that it's God speaking, but
when I do this, great ideas come to me: a small thing
I need to start doing; something I need to say to
someone; or someone I haven't called. I can write
down these ideas and consider how to put them into
action.

*Thank you for the powerful ideas that come
from meditating on your word.*

Meditation is to Scripture as digestion
is to food.

# *Becoming Still*

*But I have stilled and quieted my soul; like a
weaned child with its mother, like a weaned
child is my soul within me.*—PSALM 131:2

In times of panic, I have at least three choices:

- I can assume the worst will happen and fly into
  a frenzy.
- I can stuff myself with food or exercise myself
  into a stupor.
- I can use my tools and process my fears.

My soul can be stilled and quieted without being
force-fed. This shift from panic to serenity is not
instant. As I journal, call a friend, or go to a meeting,
my self-talk gets healthier and I cast aside my negative thinking. Soon I am at peace with myself and my
world.

*Help me to learn the skill of quieting
my soul and build it into a habit.*

I have the capacity to still and quiet
my soul, if I will.

# *Wonderful Body Shapes*

*I praise you because I am fearfully and wonderfully made; your works are wonderful. ... When I was woven together in the depths of the earth, your eyes saw my unformed body.*—PSALM 139:14, 15

I have felt ashamed of my body because it isn't shaped the way my culture says it should be. I have sized myself up and decided that no matter what size I am, it is wrong. I dread looking in the mirror. Saying my body is *wonderful* seems overstated and, quite truthfully, a lie.

It takes a while to agree with God that my body is wonderfully made. God created all types of body shapes and sizes, not preferring one over the other. A pear-shaped body is as wonderful to him as any other. My culture's preference for certain sizes and shapes over others is arbitrary. My culture's prejudice in labeling certain body shapes and sizes as misshapen and ugly violates God's truth. All body shapes and sizes are *wonderfully made* because of who made them.

*God, please take away my self-loathing for my body and replace it with self-respect.*

All body shapes and sizes are the work of God's creation.

# Grandiosity Unveiled

*Do not be wise in your own eyes.*
—PROVERBS 3:7

The word *grandiosity* means being wise in one's own eyes. I've been grandiose when I've known the answer to every dilemma, when I've thought I could solve my weight problem in a minute—if I wanted to, when I've thought I could solve everyone's problems if they did things my way.

The antidote to my grandiosity is understanding the severe limitations of being human. My compulsive eating behaviors made my limitations obvious and began shattering my grandiosity. The more I understand just how much my eating behaviors thwarted me, the more humble I feel. I am ready to acknowledge the frailness and fragility of my own humanness and surrender to the unlimited wisdom of God.

*God, keep showing me my many grandiose ideas about life.*

Getting in touch with my grandiosity
shows me my need for God.

# *Sexuality*

*May your fountain be blessed, and may you
rejoice in the wife of your youth.*
—PROVERBS 5:18

My all-or-nothing, black-and-white thinking led
me to believe these extreme myths about sexuality.

- Prudery: I didn't deserve to understand or enjoy my sexuality.
- Promiscuity: I needed to express my sexuality
casually to get people to notice or love me.

As I choose *not* to think in extremes, I can accept
that God created me to be a sexual person and I can
channel this gift appropriately. I can enjoy an appropriate sexual relationship. I can take pleasure in
dressing according to my gender without calling attention to myself.

*Help me to not run away from my sexuality
or to overindulge it, God. Help me see
it as you see it.*

Sexuality is God's gift, and I can enjoy it
as God designed it.

# The Fear of God

*The fear of the Lord is the beginning of wisdom, and knowledge of the Holy One is understanding.*—PROVERBS 9:10

People who loathe themselves as much as I have can easily misunderstand the "fear of the Lord." The fear of the Lord is not, as some would suppose, terror of a whimsical, powerful tyrant who wields thunderbolts for the fun of it. But it is also not simple awe and reverence.

It is a sensible, healthy, respectful fear for a powerful being. He is not a childish dictator, but he is also not a best pal or a permissive parent. I can barely understand God because he encompasses dimensions of justice and mercy that reach beyond human understanding. He is God, and to fear him is not to be terrified, but to respect and treat him as an all-powerful supreme being.

*God, I want to acknowledge and fear you as the powerful being you are without being so fearful of you that I can't relate to you.*

Wisdom involves understanding that God is the Holy One.

# *The Pretending Game*

*Better to be a nobody and yet have a servant
than pretend to be somebody and have no
food.*—PROVERBS 12:9

Pretending is exhausting. It robs me of my inner
resources and puts me on guard at all times. I can't
relax with others, with myself, or even with God.

Sometimes I pretend to be a more confident,
capable person. Other times I pretend to be a trouble-
maker because there's something in me that likes to
create chaos. Still other times I pretend to be quiet
and withdrawn because I'm scared of the confident
people around me. As long as I wear these masks, I
have to keep up the facade and not bare myself to
anyone.

As I admit that I am a compulsive eater, I'm free
to be just me—no more, no less. I don't need everyone to like me because the love of God and the love
of friends are calming my neediness for acceptance.

*Thank you for loving me for who I am.
Help me trust that and shed my masks.*

God and others accept me as I am,
and I can do that, too.

# The D Word: Discipline

*He who ignores discipline comes to poverty and shame, but whoever heeds correction is honored.*—PROVERBS 13:18

I don't like the word *disciplined* because it makes me think of the way I beat myself up and badger myself into doing the right thing. Then I react to my own harshness and want to overeat.

"It works if you work it," is a gentle way of saying that I can discipline myself. I do the footwork by using the tools God's given me. I need to talk with others about recovery, hearing their stories and sharing mine. I need to read the Bible and recovery literature to remind me of how I can grow. I need to find a sponsor to partner with me in this journey. These tools correct my old thinking and renew my mind. They help me look at myself and surrender to God.

*God, help me humble myself once again and take up the tools I've put down.*

Discipline is not beating myself up. It's using my tools.

# Smart Answers

*A gentle answer turns away wrath, but a harsh word stirs up anger.*—PROVERBS 15:1

"When in doubt, leave it out" is one of my mottoes now. I've decided to give up my grandiose, know-it-all attitude. I don't have to air every observation, opinion, or accusation that comes ripping through my mind.

I'm giving up clever comebacks and put-downs. They make me feel guilty afterward. If I don't come up with them, I'm tempted later to turn the conversation over and over in my mind until I do think of one.

My gentle answer turns away *my* wrath as well as everyone else's. I feel better when I'm gentle. I don't need to use food to assuage my anger and guilt, and I feel generous toward others.

*Thank you for the grace to pull back when I feel the need to run over people with my words.*

My gentle answer turns away my wrath.

# *Living in the Present*

*All the days of the oppressed are wretched,*
*but the cheerful heart has a continual*
*feast.*—PROVERBS 15:15

A continual feast is the dream of every compulsive overeater and bulimic. In its broadest sense, a continual feast is a day in which I enjoy each food that is brought before me.

In recovery a continual feast is enjoying each moment as it comes rather than worrying about the past and the future. I can continually feast in the present moment when I trust God that whatever happens will turn out for my benefit.

The people and events of today are set before me, and I can choose to enjoy them, ignore them, or complain about them. This is my choice.

*God, help me experience each moment*
*as it comes and enjoy each moment as*
*much as possible.*

Life can be something like a continual
feast if I allow it to be.

# *Separate Purposes*

*Better a meal of vegetables where there is
love than a fattened calf with hatred.*
—PROVERBS 15:17

Food and love don't mix. Their purposes are separate but I have intertwined them.

- The purpose of food is to nourish a person's body.
- The purpose of love is to nourish a person's inner self.

Even at mealtime, food doesn't create love and joy. Food simply nourishes, while love can create joy at mealtime.

I can let food serve its intended purpose to nourish my body without using it to feel loved, affirmed, or comforted. I also don't use it as a weapon for control or a way to continue the abuse my body may have suffered. I take care of my neediness for love by reaching out to God and others.

*Give me respect for food and mealtimes
for their simple purposes only.*

I can separate food from my neediness.

# When Self-Talk Goes Wild

*The heart of the righteous weighs its answers. . . .*—PROVERBS 15:28

My negative self-talk is like traffic in my head that drowns out God's promptings. I'm learning to weigh how I answer my self-talk:

- I don't have to expect the worst. I will wait and see what happens.
- I don't have to feel persecuted. No one is out to get me. I will give the other person the benefit of the doubt.
- I don't have to expect myself and others to be perfect. There is no such thing as an all-caring parent, best friend, or spouse.

God knows my heart, and he is teaching me to calm and comfort myself. He asks me to rest in his presence and helps me to quiet my anxiety.

*God, renew my mind by helping me correct my negative self-talk.*

I can answer my negative self-talk with wisdom.

# *Flexibility*

*In his heart a man plans his course, but the Lord determines his steps.*—PROVERBS 16:9

I have coped with life and with weight gains by using rigid attempts to control myself. I planned and planned and planned my food, my diets, and my life events only to find that no plan considered all the contingencies. No eating plan had my name on it.

As I give up my eating behaviors, I give up my compulsive controlling, too. I let things happen, and I ask God to help me cope with them. Every time I panic, I feel the urge to control, but I give it up again.

All plans are tentative now. I understand that God determines my steps so I make my needs known, plan a possible course, and watch with anticipation to see what will happen.

*Help me surrender to you, God,
my need to control.*

Flexibility begins with giving God my
plans.

# When Logic Fails

*There is a way that seems right to a man,
but in the end it leads to death.*
—PROVERBS 16:25

Many things that seemed logical and practical to me no longer seem so. My out-of-the-ordinary eating behaviors seemed to solve my problems of staying thin, getting rid of anger, and killing off my appetite, but they backfired. My body deteriorated, and my life became unmanageable.

My logic failed me at other times, too. I thought beating myself up would motivate me to work harder in life, but it made me feel worthless. Pretending to feel fine worked only until the next crisis occurred.

Now when something seems logical to me, I run it past God in prayer and I check it out with others. I understand that what seems right to me may turn out to be wrong, and when it is, I try to learn from it.

*Help me set aside logical conclusions
and wait for more information and
insight from you.*

Just because something seems logical
or practical doesn't make it right.

# *Confidentiality*

*He who covers over an offense promotes love,
but whoever repeats the matter separates
close friends.*—PROVERBS 17:9

Sometimes when others tell me things they've done, I get on my high horse and say, "At least I've never done that!" Then the next day I come within inches of doing something similar, so I end up confessing my judgmental attitude to God.

Slowly I'm learning not to judge people or talk about their mistakes. They are not terrible; they are like me. They're bound up in a powerful inner struggle, and they need my love and acceptance.

Besides, when I gloat about others' defects, it distracts me from my own struggling attempts to do whatever it takes to surrender my compulsive behaviors. I don't need additional distractions, so I need to forego gossip and obsessive judgment of others for my own good as well.

*God, thank you that others trust me to love
them the way you love me. Help me to keep
attempting to do that.*

Confidentiality means I shelter other's
secrets from outsiders and from my own
prideful judgments.

# *Taking Life Less Seriously*

*A cheerful heart is good medicine, but a crushed spirit dries up the bones.*
—PROVERBS 17:22

Recovering from an eating disorder is not a gloom-and-doom experience. In my support group I'm learning to laugh about how paranoid and panicky I am in my eating disorder. At first, all that laughter in those groups seems strange, but the laughter is part of surrendering to God and admitting powerlessness. It's how compulsive people identify with one another and accept one another.

Now that I feel more accepted, I don't worry so much about how I look when I make mistakes. I can even laugh at old pictures of myself. I'm not so self-conscious about what I draw, write, cook, or build. So what if it's not perfect? Neither am I.

Laughing at my mistakes tells myself and others that I have let go of the controls. What a relief!

*Thank you, God, for helping me take myself less seriously and your interest in me very seriously.*

I take myself too seriously when I'm my only hope.

# *Balanced Thinking*

*A discerning man keeps wisdom in view,
but a fool's eyes wander to the ends
of the earth.*—PROVERBS 17:24

It's possible to wander off into a completely spiritual or psychological approach to recovery without respect for the way my body works and metabolizes food. I can fool myself into thinking:

- If I work through all my issues, it won't matter if I eat a lot of high-fat foods.
- If I pray every day, it won't matter if I never exercise (or exercise too much).

Respect for the workings of my body means that I abide by accepted general principles of exercise and nutrition and I put them into practice without becoming obsessed by them. When I ignore them, I'm in the same kind of denial I was in before my eating disorder. I'm buying into magical thinking because I don't want to do necessary, but difficult, things.

*God, show me how I can use exercise and
nutrition properly to energize and care for
my body without beating myself up.*

If I don't want to be rigorously honest,
I need to ask myself why.

# Listening Well

*He who answers before listening—that is his
folly and his shame.*—PROVERBS 18:13

The no-crosstalk rule used in support groups
(for more explanation, see glossary) works well in
relationships, too. When I don't allow myself to interrupt, others have a chance to say what they feel. As
they wander around in their thoughts, they eventually spit out what they think. And I'm glad I gave them
time because now I know them better.

I don't rush in anymore—to rescue with answers,
to defend my position, or to stop the flow of tears. I
also try not to analyze or talk back in my thoughts. I
try to give all my attention to listening. I allow people
to be themselves, and I respect them with my silence.

*God, help me value others the way you do—
by listening to them with no worry of how
much they do or don't make sense.*

When I silence the traffic in my head,
I hear more of what others
are trying to say.

# *To Be Unoffendable*

*A man's wisdom gives him patience; it is his glory to overlook an offense.*—PROVERBS 19:11

When someone offends me, it's no longer a major event in my life. I don't have to dwell on it or analyze how much they meant to insult me. I don't have to rehearse how I can confront them. I'm learning to give up the offense and overlook it. Even if it was intended, I can temper my conclusions with mercy.

People who overlook offenses are easy to be with. They don't misunderstand me and misinterpret what I say as a negative comment about them. I don't have to go back and say, "I hope you didn't think I meant. . . ." At first I mistook this positive nature as naivety and weakness, but now I see it as serenity and strength. I want the same thing for myself.

*Help me, God, give grace to others*
*as you give grace to me.*

Whether I choose to be offended says
more about me than the other person.

# Drawing Others Out

*The purposes of a man's heart are deep
waters, but a man of understanding draws
them out.*—PROVERBS 20:5

I'm learning to ask more questions and give fewer answers. I see my defects of character so clearly now that I know I'm not a fountain of wisdom anymore.

Now I have a lot more faith in people's ability to understand themselves. They sit in support groups and talk through issues that have puzzled them for years—with no help from me!

When people ask my advice or my opinion, I'm more likely to draw them out now. I pose questions. I reflect their feelings back to them. Then I ask that tough question: What do you think God wants you to do?

*Help me draw others out instead
of spout off what I know.*

I help others more by helping them
help themselves.

# *Moody Blues*

*Better to live on a corner of the roof than
share a house with a quarrelsome wife.*
—PROVERBS 21:9

When I felt quarrelsome, even I didn't like living
with myself. The feeling of grouchiness loomed over
me—and everyone else—like a threatening cloud
from which no one could escape.

Admitting to myself that I have a problem with
grouchiness gives me the desire to surrender it. Frequently I journal about it or call someone to avoid
spreading it within my family and co-workers. Facing the problem also helps me get at the root of my
grouchy feelings of fear, anger, or self-pity so I can
surrender them.

I see now why someone would rather sit on a
roof in all kinds of weather rather than be around me
when I'm brooding. As my moody moments become
less frequent, others want to be around me more.

*God, please rid me of the grouchiness that
seems to stick to me like wet clothing.*

I can choose whether I will nurse my
moodiness or confront it.

# *Cravings*

*The sluggard's craving will be the death
of him, because his hands refuse to work.
All day long he craves for more. . . .*
—PROVERBS 21:25–26

I have been so focused on eating and not eating that I have ignored my health, my goals, and my dreams. I have felt guilty for giving in to my cravings and I've told myself I'd never amount to anything anyway, so why try? I've daydreamed and fantasized about food, so I've sacrificed the good things I wanted to do. There wasn't time to read a book or see a friend—I had to find a store and buy some ice cream.

Now that I'm surrendering these cravings to God, I have time for life. I make appointments with the doctor when I need to; I build relationships with those I previously envied for their smaller size; I need less time to snack so I have more time to enjoy gardening or playing volleyball.

*God, help me see facets of life open
to me as I shut the door on my cravings.*

As I get rid of my cravings, I can
"get a life."

# *Excuses*

*The sluggard says, "There is a lion outside!"*
*or, "I will be murdered in the streets!"*
—PROVERBS 22:13

Just as a lazy person makes excuses for not going to work, I have my reasons for my strange relationship with food.

- I am overweight because I'm big-boned.
- Dieting (or binging and purging) gives me control.
- It's good for me to snack or skip meals.

As I face the truth about myself in light of God's abundant love for me, I can admit the truth: I am obsessed with food; I am obsessed with thinness.

There is no lion outside. The lion is within me, driving me to be compulsive. As I relinquish my excuses and admit the truth about myself, I am opening the doors of my house and rushing outside. With God's help, I have hope and courage to tame the lion within me.

*God, help me admit the excuses and*
*cover-ups I've been using*
*for my eating behaviors.*

My compulsive eating behaviors come
from within, not from without.

# *Enthusiasm*

*There is surely a future hope for you,*
*and your hope will not be cut off.*
—PROVERBS 23:18

Will anything ever get better? Will I ever amount
to anything? What can be expected from a compulsive person?

My great fears about my future being "cut off"
were normal for someone with an eating disorder.
Nothing seemed to work. But now I'm surrendering
myself to God, which gives me hope because he has
the power to change me.

To be hopeful feels good and presents the possi-
bility of being enthusiastic once again. The word
*enthusiasm* comes from the two Latin words *en* and
*theos* meaning "in God." When I remain "in God,"
I have every reason to be filled with hope and anticipation about my future.

*Thank you, God, for giving me a future*
*and a hope.*

Enthusiasm is the child of hope.

# Refining My Abstinence

*If you find honey, eat just enough—too much of it, and you will vomit.*—PROVERBS 25:16

My abstinence is a living, growing thing. Some foods are like honey; they are fine as long as I don't have too much of them. When I start daydreaming about certain foods, I abstain from them. When I become obsessive about weighing myself, I ask someone to hide the scales for a month.

Rigorous honesty demands that I eliminate from my life the foods and eating behaviors that drive me. It's tempting to rationalize that they are not a problem, but the more I see the benefits of abstinence, the more quickly I identify those driven things and abstain from them.

I don't consider that I'm depriving myself, but that I'm focusing my energies on the best things in life: relationships, work, and knowledge of God's will.

*Please help me, God, recognize my driven behaviors and abstain from them.*

Committing my abstinence to God means listening to him about how it needs to be refined.

# *Others' Boundaries*

*Seldom set foot in your neighbor's house—*
*too much of you, and he will hate you.*
—PROVERBS 25:17

Setting foot in my neighbor's house is fine as long as she wants it that way. She's prepared to talk for a while and give me refreshment if I need it. This is delightful, but I won't expect her to do it again tomorrow or the next day.

I'm learning to respect the boundaries of others. I don't dump my thoughts or feelings on people who aren't equipped to hear them. Even with close friends, I don't go on and on about myself.

When I involve other people in my recovery, I respect their boundaries of time and privacy. I'm grateful for what they give me, and I don't demand more or feel disappointed when they aren't able to give more.

*Thank you, God, for the people you've sent to love me, and help me treat them with respect.*

People find it easier to love me when
I don't expect so much of them.

# *Confession Prospers*

*He who conceals his sins does not prosper,*
*but whoever confesses and renounces them*
*finds mercy.*—PROVERBS 28:13

Concealing my eating disorder was important. I felt that if people knew about it, they wouldn't like me.

Now I find that admitting the disgusting behaviors of my eating disorder opens me to God's mercy. I share them in my support group and hang my head, feeling as if no one will ever speak to me again. But I look up to find others nodding in agreement. What relief! Others know the truth about me and still accept me. Their attitude of pardon "puts skin on God," and I feel even more assured that I am forgiven.

These new attitudes of honesty and transparency prosper me. They allow me to be intimate in a healthy way, to quit trying to impress people, and to admit my mistakes with candor. I feel freer than I ever have to be the person God created me to be.

*Thank you, God, for showing me that*
*openness and humility lead to wholeness.*

Sharing my secrets in a safe environment
helps me grow.

# *Obsessed with Thinness*

> *Fear of man will prove to be a snare, but whoever trusts in the Lord is kept safe.*
> —PROVERBS 29:25

Trying to please others is impossible, but I thought I was a Superperson so I tried. When it didn't work, I ate. Then I found that no matter how much I dieted, there was no pleasing the cultural standard of thinness.

Nothing satisfies my culture except a pencil-thin and tummy-tucked body. Some movie stars use body doubles for distant shots; others use body doubles for close-up shots. Yet I berate myself because my body will never conform to that perfect body image that even movie stars don't achieve.

That image is not worth achieving. It's safer to trust God to show me the goal weight that is best for me and to help me find the necessary abstinence to achieve it. Unlike our culture, God doesn't hold it against me if it takes me a while to do this.

*God, please keep me focused on becoming a whole person and help me avoid becoming obsessed with thinness.*

My goal is to return to a normal weight for my body—no more, no less.

# *Hooked on Productivity*

*There was no end to his toil, yet his eyes
were not content on his wealth.*
—ECCLESIASTES 4:8

Work is generally a good thing unless it becomes compulsive. Alongside my eating disorder, I feel the urge to prove myself to the world. I do this by:

- being a compulsive volunteer, saying "yes" to whatever is asked of me, and making sure I do the best job that's ever been done for that task;
- finding my "career path" and hiking down that path faster and farther than anyone who has gone before me;
- hurrying my life away doing twenty things at once; and
- feeling good only when I accomplish many or all the things on my daily checklist.

I can surrender this, too, because it is no different from my eating disorder in its frenzied attempt to fill my neediness.

*God, help me see the similarity between my
eating disorder and the other things in life
that drive me.*

Compulsive working looks more
respectable but is no less debilitating
than an eating disorder.

# *I Can Do It Myself!*

*Two are better than one, because they have a good return for their work.*—ECCLESIASTES 4:9

Everything within me convinces me that I can beat my eating disorder alone. I, the "lone ranger," have never needed anyone. Who says I need someone now? Why should I have to drive across town to a silly support-group meeting? What do those people know that I don't?

It's not what those people know, it's what they are. I need to be around them to see that I am one of many with an eating disorder. I need to hear their stories to confirm within myself that I am not crazy. I need to share at the meeting so I can hear words come out of my own mouth about why I want to change. I need to hear others' words echo over the next few days as I face the eating-disorder tiger in myself.

I need those people, and they need me; God made it that way.

*God, help me humble myself enough
to reach out to go to a meeting.*

Isolation is a symptom of pride
and grandiosity; reaching out is a sign
of surrender.

# *Asking for Help*

*If one falls down, his friend can help him up.*
*But pity the man who falls and has no one*
*to help him up!*—ECCLESIASTES 4:10

Before friends can help me up, I have to notify
them that I've fallen down. Sometimes I have trouble
with that. Asking for help assumes that I am a valued
person, and I'm just beginning to believe that. Asking
for help means I have to trust someone, and I'm just
beginning to trust others.

But at times I gather my courage and call a friend
on the telephone, and when I do, I am helped so
much. I hear my angry and hurt thoughts expressed
aloud, and I release them. I hear my eager and determined thoughts become audible words, and I renew
my courage to go on.

I hang up the telephone feeling as if I'm starting
a new day. I'm excited about what is to come.

*Please give me courage to make a telephone*
*call to a friend when I need support.*

Friendship is not a luxury, but a necessity
in facing an eating disorder.

# *Accountability Works*

*Though one may be overpowered, two can defend themselves. A cord of three strands is not quickly broken.*—ECCLESIASTES 4:12

When I make myself accountable to others, I wrap a strong protective cord around me. I can go back to my life knowing that I'm safely tethered to others, and that tether provides strength.

I, who lack willpower, am now empowered by my partnership with others. Knowing that they stand beside me in my efforts to surrender my compulsiveness, rage, and self-pity makes me stand taller. I don't give in so quickly because it's more than just me who's fighting this thing.

The intense look in their eyes and the serious set of their jaws tell me that I can depend on them to be strong when I am weak.

*God, help me humble myself enough to make myself accountable as often as I need to.*

Accountability empowers.

# *Risky Business*

*Cast your bread upon the waters, for after
many days you will find it again.*
—ECCLESIASTES 11:1

It is risky, even absurd, to throw food away. But
God tells me that if I risk enough to surrender my
food to him, he will bring it back to me in my time
of need. When it does come back it is in the form of
spiritual bread. I am ready to receive it because I'm
making more room in my life for it.

Faith is a risky business. I must believe enough
in God's love to trust him to give me what I need,
even though it looks as if I'm giving up exactly what
I need.

But it is exciting. I give up food, and God sus-
tains me. I give up the need to impress others, and
God impresses them for me. I give up control, and
God controls events better than I ever could.

*God, help me move down this risky path
of surrender.*

Recovery is the wisest risk I can take
and will yield the greatest returns.

# From the Inside Out

*How beautiful you are and how pleasing,*
*O love, with your delights!*
—SONG OF SONGS 7:6

No matter how many compliments I receive on my appearance, I can name many things wrong with it. My face is not clear enough, my hair looks scruffy, my hips—don't even talk about them.

The woman to whom today's verse was spoken may or may not have been a knockout beauty, but the love and positive flow between her lover and her created her beauty. This helps me see that my attitudes can make me more attractive.

For example, I am more attractive when I take it easy on myself. My face and gestures relax and a genuine smile lights up my face. I accept myself to the point that I enjoy working on my appearance. I understand that being attractive comes from inner peace as well as the peace I've made with the looks that the Creator God gave me.

*God, help me become attractive*
*from the inside out.*

My body becomes as attractive
as my attitudes.

# *Life as a Problem Solver*

*"Come now, let us reason together," says the Lord. "Though your sins are like scarlet, they shall be as white as snow; though they are red as crimson, they shall be like wool."*
—ISAIAH 1:18

I used to say to food, "Let us escape together over problems." God says to me, "Let us reason together over solutions."

I want to be solution-oriented, too. For too long I have muddled over problems by blaming others and escaping in food. It feels different to solve a problem the way I tackle a jigsaw puzzle. I am learning to allay my initial panic and examine the problem from all sides. I commit myself to stay with it until I figure out the puzzle or find someone who can.

*I praise you, God, the tackler*
*of great problems.*

Maturity means working
through problems.

# *Out of the Darkness*

*The people walking in darkness have seen
a great light; on those living in the land
of the shadow of death a light has
dawned.*—ISAIAH 9:2

Facing my eating disorder transforms me. My thinking and my way of life are different. I change from one who walks in the darkness of panic to one who walks in the light of serenity. I'm escaping from the "shadow of death" of the junk-food malnutrition and high blood pressure that could have robbed me of life. I may still struggle, but I am being freed. I'm emerging wounded yet wise, surrendered yet strong.

In Isaiah's day, the nation of Judah was losing its integrity and national strength, but God worked with Judah and turned the nation into an instrument for him. He is doing the same thing with me. He's done it before; I can trust him to keep doing it with me.

*Thank you, God, that with you
anything is possible.*

Living without my eating disorder can
become a reality in my life.

# The Drive
# to Feel Good

*The Sovereign Lord will wipe away the tears
from all faces; he will remove the disgrace
of his people from all the earth.*—ISAIAH 25:8

When I read words like those in the verse above,
I want to shout, "When? When? When?" I know that
God won't wipe away sorrow until the next life, but I
keep hoping for something sooner.

I have felt so driven to feel good that I've tried to
use an eating disorder to achieve it. I'm not good at
sitting with my hurt and enduring it. I want to take
the soft, easy way, not the long, difficult one.

I am learning that some things are more important than feeling good—serenity, treating others fairly,
fulfilling God's purposes for me, and staying abstinent even if it feels miserable. So I go along with this
new approach and look forward to the feel-good days
of the future.

*Please help me set aside the desire to feel
good all the time and take up new desires
for serenity and purpose.*

My goal is long-term contentment,
not a quick fix.

# *Steady Serenity*

*You will keep in perfect peace him whose
mind is steadfast, because he trusts in you.*
—ISAIAH 26:3

When I haven't been pleased with the circumstances and people in my life, I've tried to control them. For a while, I got what I wanted, but it forced me to be more controlling. The more I tried to manage my world, the more compulsive I became. What is repeated fad dieting, bulimia, or anorexia but weight control gone mad?

Serenity is based on having a steady mind even when I cannot control anything around me. It is a renewed mind that rejects the myths of my culture that money, fame, or thinness will make me "good enough." It's a refocused mind that doesn't chase after more and more things to try to be happy.

I can let go of control and let God direct things. I can agree with God that he has given me everything I need.

*God, I trust you to take control.*

The more I trust God, the more
I learn serenity.

# *Mixed Motives*

*These people . . . honor me with their lips,
but their hearts are far from me.*
—ISAIAH 29:13

For years I've said the right words and done the
right things, but with questionable motives. I've
helped people because I didn't want to feel guilty or
because I didn't want to upset them. All that guilt and
maneuvering played into my eating disorder, and I
paid for each mixed motive with candy bars, french
fries, and third helpings at dinner.

It's important to sort out my motives. If I stop
doing things just because I feel guilty, what will I stop
doing? What encouraging words will I stop offering
simply to get people to like me?

Not until I stop doing things with mixed motives
can I unearth my positive motives. Then I can be free
to be caring and kind from a full heart.

*Help me have a pure heart, God,
and to acknowledge when I don't.*

I force my eating disorder to pay
for doing things I don't want to do.

# Strength in Quietness

*In repentance and rest is your salvation,*
*in quietness and trust is your strength. . . .*
—ISAIAH 30:15

Just as I'm learning to open up and talk, I'm learning to be quiet, too.

Sometimes I free myself of my frustration by sharing it with recovering friends, but other times it's better to sit with it and be quiet. I've harped on it long enough, and I've learned all I can. Now it's time to wait because it's beyond my control and I can't change it by talking about it. Perhaps I will learn more from waiting on it than from talking about it.

It's not a gagged silence. It's a voluntary one in which I trust that something is going to occur if I simply leave things alone. As I turn it over to God, I release it and watch what happens.

*God, help me simmer down and trust you.*

Being quiet cuts through the traffic
in my mind and helps me listen to what
God may be saying.

# *Beating Myself Up*

*Forget the former things; do not dwell
on the past.*—ISAIAH 43:18

Part of what has fed my compulsion has been beating myself up for the things I've done wrong in the past. I've dwelt on the many unkind things I've thought and said and the unwise decisions I've made.

God didn't beat up the nation of Judah, heaping blame and shame on them, although they had been faithless. He urged them not to dwell on their past failures and challenged them to move ahead.

He follows the same path with me, which helps me see the futility of beating myself up. Yes, I've made mistakes. But I seek forgiveness, make amends when possible, and go on. I believe that God can change me into a different person.

*God, give me the strength to forgive myself
and others and move on.*

God focuses on what can be done
in the present instead of dwelling on what
I should have done in the past.

# *Becoming Adventurous*

*See, I am doing a new thing! Now it springs
up; do you not perceive it?*—ISAIAH 43:19

Can I let God do something new in my life? Can I set aside my fears and step out? New things in life scared me because I didn't know enough about them to control them. I wasn't skilled enough at them to be sure that they would build up my faltering self-esteem.

Now that I'm addressing these issues, I am freer to try new things. I can learn to serve a volleyball. I can take art lessons. I can speak in front of others. I can make friends with someone who doesn't talk about food and diets. I can eat *good* foods (like brussels sprouts) without disgust and *bad* foods (like butter on my toast) without guilt.

When I experiment, I may stumble upon one more piece of God's will for me.

*God, show me your paths and give me
the courage to follow them—even if they look
new to me.*

When I try something new, I can allay
my fears and dabble in serenity.

# *Overreacting to Criticism*

*Hear me, you who know what is right. . . . Do not fear the reproach of men or be terrified by their insults.*—ISAIAH 51:7

I react to other people's criticisms in extreme ways. Sometimes I assume they must be true because I'm so inadequate, so I whip myself until I'm bloodied.

Other times I defend myself on and on until I'm sure I've convinced them that their criticisms aren't true (or perhaps I've just convinced them that I'm defensive). Afterward, I continue to rehearse my defense-attorney speech, and they rehearse the reasons they never want to talk to me again.

I'm finally learning to listen to critics, thank them, and go on. Then I ask myself if the criticism is useful. I sit on it a few days, and sometimes God brings to my mind instances in which the criticism was true. Other times I figure out that it is not true and I forget it.

*God, help me stop overreacting to criticism.*

I can decide if a criticism is valid
and respond appropriately.

# *The Shame of the Past*

*Do not be afraid; you will not suffer shame.
Do not fear disgrace; you will not be
humiliated. You will forget the shame
of your youth....* —ISAIAH 54:4

I relive some of the events of my past because I feel such shame about them. Some are foolish things I did when I was younger, and I regret them because I know I deeply hurt people. As I make amends and forgive myself, the shame goes away.

Other shameful events were not my fault, but I felt shamed anyway because people were hostile toward me. In some instances I confront those who mistreated me and created this shame. In other instances, I accept that they are bound up in shame themselves. I start working at forgiving these people.

I need someone as powerful as God to release me from my shame. As I surrender each shameful event to him, he releases the humiliation from them. I don't feel the sting of the shame so keenly.

*I surrender the shame of my past
to you, God*

I work through my past with the purpose
of releasing the shame.

# Side-by-Side Shepherding

*They are shepherds who lack understanding;
they all turn to their own way, each seeks his
own gain.*—ISAIAH 56:11

As a recovering *fixer*, I have tried to shepherd
people without understanding their problems. In ret-
rospect I see that I was simply trying to get them to
do things my way. My gain was the subtle grandiosity
of managing others' lives often, mixed with healthy
attitudes of wanting to help them.

I'm abandoning this savior complex and choosing instead to walk beside others as they experience
struggles. I offer no answers, although I may offer my
experience, strength, and hope. I pursue *shepherding*
and sponsoring relationships that are mutually helpful, and I share my mistakes readily.

This way involves less work and is more enjoyable. I see why it works.

*God, please place me as a shepherd in the
relationships in which you want me, but keep
me from fixing.*

Part of helping others is respecting them.

# God's Work of Art

*Yet, O Lord, you are our Father. We are the clay, you are the potter; we are all the work of your hand.*—ISAIAH 64:8

I am a work of art and nothing less. My value comes from the fact that I am made by the earth's creator, and he is my father. It's true that I don't always do everything right, but God expects me to make mistakes and loves me anyway.

If I focus only on how the world views me, I will feel worthless and unacceptable. When I understand that I am the work of God's hand, I see that my disappointments and setbacks are used by God to turn me into a one-of-a-kind container.

I believe that God has a use for me even though I may not be aware of it. As his plan unfolds, I commit myself to enjoying him more and abandoning my eating disorder.

*Thank you for creating me with such care.*

I am God's work of art.

# *Hooked on Control*

*With his mouth each speaks cordially
to his neighbor, but in his heart he sets a trap
for him.*—JEREMIAH 9:8

Controlling others takes many forms such as coercing, manipulating, shaming, flattering, and talking behind people's backs. I trap them into becoming the people I think they should be because I think I know what is best for them. If I'm successful, I may force them to detour from the person God wants them to be. I am not surprised that they become irritated.

Recovering from my eating disorder involves giving up control over my friends, relatives, and especially those to whom I am an authority figure. I go the extra mile to avoid controlling my children or those I supervise. I present desired behaviors and consequences, and I administer consequences when necessary. But I can never crawl into their hearts and change them. Only God can do that.

*I surrender my compulsive controlling to you,
Lord. You can be in charge.*

I can enjoy others more if I leave them
with their freedom of choice intact.

# A Recovering
# Know-It-All

*Let not the wise man boast of his wisdom or
the strong man boast of his strength or the
rich man boast of his riches, but let him who
boasts boast about this: that he understands
and knows me.*—JEREMIAH 9:23–24

I got myself into my eating-disorder behavior by
thinking that I knew it all about eating and weight
control. Even though it's apparent to me that my wisdom and strength are small, I still get the idea that I
have the answer. I think I can solve all my problems
myself.

When I surrender, I admit that none of my grandiose ideas work. I admit that I'm not holding out for
one more miracle diet or dazzling self-help book to
relieve my problem. I admit that only God, a power
greater than myself, can remove my compulsion.

This surrender weaves itself throughout my life.
Because I know I'm not an expert, I listen to others
more. Because I'm no longer my own god, I find it easier to worship God.

*I surrender my need to be wise
and clever to you, God.*

Knowing it all kills; surrendering
it all renews.

# Growing in Confidence

> *But blessed is the man who trusts in the Lord, whose confidence is in him. He will be like a tree planted by the water that sends out its roots by the stream. It does not fear. . . . It has no worries in a year of drought and never fails to bear fruit.*
> —JEREMIAH 17:7–8

My fears are many; I fear abandonment and intimacy; I fear failure and success. I have backed off from friendships in fear of rejection.

Because I'm choosing to trust in God, I can be confident. My roots are deeper now; I know that my confidence is rooted in how God values me. My years of drought are less panicky; I'm learning to cope with things I cannot control. My seasons of bearing fruit are lengthening; God is using me in ways that amaze me. I am growing in the confidence I've wished for all my life.

*Help me give each fear to you, God.*

I am not a person of great confidence,
but I have great confidence in God.

# *Hope for the Future*

*"For I know the plans I have for you,"*
*declares the Lord, "plans to prosper you and*
*not to harm you, plans to give you hope*
*and a future."*—JEREMIAH 29:11

The ups and downs of my eating disorder convinced me that there was little hope for my future. As I turn myself over to God, the veil of lies I've been telling myself is lifting and I can see ahead.

Now I see that when everything is crumbling around me, I can cling to the fact that God has given me a future and a hope. He actually has plans for me—the one who has been enslaved to an eating disorder. Nothing is hopeless with God, not even the worst circumstances.

Jeremiah spoke the words in today's verse to people who would be taken captive, but even they had a future and a hope. That means that there is always a reason to get up tomorrow, a reason to get dressed, a reason to plan my day. God will work, and my hope will be rewarded.

*God, help me to believe in this hope for the*
*future that you have given me.*

God supplies hope when I have no hope.

# *Letting Go of Fatigue*

*Then maidens will dance and be glad, young
men and old as well. I will turn their
mourning into gladness.*—JEREMIAH 31:13

Sometimes I feel guilty when I celebrate my progress. Life has been such serious business that I'm more comfortable feeling tense and fatigued!

I've learned that I can respond to tension by listing the things I am thankful for. I am thankful that I admit I have a problem with food, that I am not alone in my struggle, and that I surrender my anger and fears to God.

This helps me relax. Although I'm not the person I want to be, I'm not the person I once was. I can pause to think about how exciting this is. The pages of my journal show how much I've changed. I am making a turnaround from mourning to gladness.

*God, help me let go of the fatigue
and tension of the past.*

Gratefulness soothes my fatigue.

# *Personal Boundary Lines*

*"But I will rescue you on that day," declares
the Lord; "you will not be handed over to
those you fear. I will save you; you will not
fall by the sword but will escape with your
life, because you trust in me," declares the
Lord.*—JEREMIAH 39:17–18

I feel as if I need to be rescued when I am around
those who violate my boundaries. I don't like insist-
ing that others respect my choices or feeling as if they
are living their lives through me. Some people expect
me to reveal feelings and thoughts inappropriate to
our relationship, and I feel invaded.

I need God's help to stand up for myself and
assert my independence. It's as if I need a giant wres-
tler to be my guardian angel. I call on God, take a
deep breath, and assert myself politely. Others aren't
always pleased when I do this, but I am learning to
respect myself and keep the boundaries of my familiarity with others intact.

*God, help me to treat others appropriately
and to be unafraid to request the same
of them.*

To respect my own boundaries
is to respect myself and shed
my eating disorder.

# *Insomnia Blues*

*Arise, cry out in the night, as the watches of the night begin; pour out your heart like water in the presence of the Lord.*
—LAMENTATIONS 2:19

I used to view sleeplessness as an intruder, and I would eat a snack or take a pill to make myself drowsy again. Now I listen to what's going on inside myself without panicking that I won't get enough sleep to be fresh the next day.

These moments often flourish into heart-to-heart conversations with God about what I need to do or what I can't do anything about. I bring these things to him, and under the cover of darkness, I am free to cry and say my piece.

I'm trying to make friends with my insomnia by using wakeful moments as a valuable time of peace and silence to pray about things I never have time to pray about. Sometimes, in this grand state of peace, sleep sneaks up on me.

*Help me not to resent sleeplessness*
*but to use it.*

God will nurture me even through
the night if I let him.

# Every Morning Is New

*Because of the Lord's great love we are not
consumed, for his compassions never fail.
They are new every morning; great is your
faithfulness.*—LAMENTATIONS 3:22–23

Morning can be a friend. I wake up with the
energy I couldn't find when I went to bed. I have an
opportunity to start over. My slate is clean, and I can
begin again. My problems of yesterday are just that—
problems of yesterday.

This isn't just wishful, sunshine thinking. This is
reality. A piece of my old self has died in the night
and I have been restored. Now is my chance to commit my eating plan to God and see how much serenity I can live in today. This is one of many ways that
God gives me grace.

*Thank you, God, for times to start over.*

God's grace allows me to start over
whenever I need to.

# *Self-Examination*

*Let us examine our ways and test them, and let us return to the Lord.*—LAMENTATIONS 3:40

Eating compulsively seemed necessary to me because I wasn't good at facing reality, especially my character defects. As I make a searching and fearless moral inventory of myself, I discover the root character defects that cause my problems: self-pity, resentment, laziness, and fear of rejection. These defects tainted my attitudes and diminished my opportunities for relationships and career advancement. I used them to survive just as I used my eating disorder. Yet they hurt me when I thought they were helping me.

In order to maintain a clean abstinence, I surrender these character defects. I can clear my conscience today by confessing these defects and beginning to work through them.

*God, show me the ways my character defects trip me up and how they make it difficult to follow your will.*

The path to normal eating patterns is through a cleared conscience.

# Trials in the Mind

*O Lord, you took up my case; you redeemed
my life. . . . You have seen the depth of their
vengeance, all their plots against me.*
—LAMENTATIONS 3:58, 60

I am haunted by destructive, negative thoughts
that tell me I am doomed to be compulsive, I am ugly,
or I am not good at anything. If I stop listening to lies
and call on God to help me fight the battle, he says,
"Your life can be changed. You are beautiful the way
I created you. You are a significant person."

I need to hear these truths over and over. I need
for God to act as my persuasive lawyer and sway me,
the judge, into believing that I should not be condemned and locked away. Even when I dig up my past
and spread it across my mind, God can banish it with
the thought that he has redeemed my past.

*Rescue me from destructive thoughts.*

Compulsive behavior can be short-
circuited by focusing on the truth.

# *Parental Legacies?*

*But suppose this son has a son who sees all
the sins his father commits, and though he
sees them, he does not do such things. . . .*
—EZEKIEL 18:14, 17

If my parents overeat, am I doomed to overeat or
will I betray them by not overeating? Am I doomed to
purge and starve? If my parents are obsessed with
thinness, can I be otherwise?

I have many of the positive and negative qualities of my parents. Although the pull is strong to be
like them, I can choose to look at life differently. God
sees me as a separate person from my parents. I can
choose the kind of person I want to be and ask him
to help me become that person.

> *God, please help me set aside lifelong
> tendencies that block wholeness.*

I choose for myself who I will become.

# *Dry Bones Can Live*

> ... I saw a great many bones on the floor
> of the valley, bones that were very dry.
> [God] asked me, "Son of man, can
> these bones live?"—EZEKIEL 37:2–3

Even with an eating disorder, I appeared to be such a together person. I wanted to be that, and I pretended to be that. Inside I was a valley of dry bones. I was worn out from trying to fill the desperate neediness within me. None of the food I was stuffing myself with could nourish those bones. Attending support-group meetings was my way of asking, "Can these bones live?"

The prophet Ezekiel obeyed God's instructions to preach to the bones even though it sounded ridiculous. In the same way, I am exposing my broken body and heart to words of hope. As I write a moral inventory and make amends, the bones come together and tendons and flesh appear. God is waking me from my grieving state as I begin to live again.

*God, thank you for not giving up on me.*

With God's power, even the driest of lives
can be revived.

# *A Choice Abstinence*

*But Daniel resolved not to defile himself with
the royal food and wine. . . .*—DANIEL 1:8

Daniel, a spiritual person (he was later arrested
for praying three times a day!), determined that his
abstinence would include vegetables and water. Even
though it was inconvenient, he found a way to follow it.

Choosing my own abstinence is full of possibilities for rationalizations, but it is still my choice.
With God's help, I can choose a wise abstinence that
speaks to the drivenness of my compulsion. In time,
he leads me to refine and change my abstinence as I
need to. I trust him to show me what to do and to
help me see when I'm kidding myself.

*God, you know my eating disorder behaviors
better than anyone else. Please show me
the best eating plan.*

Choosing my own abstinence is a risky
but wise step in my growth.

# *Choosing Foods Wisely*

> *At the end of ten days they looked healthier and better nourished than any of the young men who ate the royal food. So the guard took away their choice food and the wine they were to drink and gave them vegetables instead.*—DANIEL 1:15–16

As I practice abstinence, mealtime is no longer the highlight of my day. I don't need my favorite foods to satisfy me because food is no longer a reward. I want to eat nutritious food for lunch so I can be more alert afterward.

It is a miracle that alertness is becoming more important than my appetite! I remember days when nothing was more important than appetite. There is hope for me yet!

*Thank you, God, for the gift of food, and help me use it to help my body function well.*

I eat simply to nourish my body—
imagine that!

# Dark Memories

*He reveals deep and hidden things;*
*he knows what lies in darkness, and light*
*dwells with him.*—DANIEL 2:22

As I face my eating disorder, I remember events from childhood and adolescence that disturb me and explain my neediness. I remember how my compulsion first began, and I feel sad. I trust God to reveal these things as I need to know them and show me the value of remembering them.

Even though some events are dark and painful, I view them now through the light of what I can learn from them. When I share them with others, I do so to overcome the hold they may still have on me. I don't blame anyone, but I want to know what kinds of things cause me to turn to food for survival. I don't have to be scared by these memories because I trust that God is the one who reveals them to me and I can ask him to help me view them with his wisdom.

*God, help me see the pain in my past that*
*has driven me to eat. Please free me from it.*

God is more powerful than my past.

# *In the Fire*

*Look! I see four men walking around in the fire, unbound and unharmed, and the fourth looks like a son of the gods.*—DANIEL 3:25

The fourth man walking through the fire with Shadrach, Meshach, and Abednego is the same man that walks through my fires with me—Jesus Christ. Just as they walked in a fiery furnace without being burned, I am learning to walk through the fires of life without being overwhelmed.

Sometimes I wish God would simply snatch me out of the fire, and at times miraculous coincidences remove me from fiery situations. But I know that my wish is part of my old tendency to escape unpleasant things. Recovery means walking through the fire and surviving. Perhaps that's an even greater miracle.

*Thank you, God, for walking with me through problems.*

I walk through problems,
not around them.

# *Roadblocks*

*Therefore I will block her path with
thornbushes; I will wall her in so that she
cannot find her way.*—HOSEA 2:6

God has a way of hedging me in so that the
wrong choices aren't available to me in some of my
neediest moments. This happens when there is no-
where to buy food, no bathroom private enough to
throw up in, or no way out of eating dinner with
someone.

At first I feel frantic when I cannot find what I
*need* to practice my compulsion. Then I feel as if God
is winking at me and saying, "Stay abstinent for just
ten minutes more, and you'll be OK." So I hang on
for ten more minutes praying or calling a friend, and
I'm OK.

As I look back on these hedged-in moments, I
see God's grace at work. I was weak, but he was strong.

*God, thank you for seeing ahead of me down
the road and preparing roadblocks when
I need them.*

Some of my roadblocks are gifts from God.

# Choices in Rage

*I will not carry out my fierce anger, nor will I
turn and devastate Ephraim. For I am God,
and not man—the Holy One among you.
I will not come in wrath.*—HOSEA 11:8–9

When I feel the rage well up inside me, it's as if
I have no choice. It must be expressed, and usually
toward the person who angers me. This verse shows
me the inner struggle of God with his own rage.
Ephraim (the nation of Israel) turned her back on
God, which made God angry. Yet God chose not to
"come in wrath."

I can make a choice similar to his. As I feel the
rage well up inside me, I can choose to punish the
person who deserves it or I can set the rage aside. I
can determine the wisest course of action and pursue
that. With my human limitations, however, I may
have to get away to vent my anger in a healthy way so
I can make my choice with a clear mind.

*Thank you, God, for showing me your inner
struggle with your own anger.*

I can choose to imitate my heavenly
parent, God, whose anger
is not destructive.

# God's Compassion

> Return to the Lord your God, for he is
> gracious and compassionate, slow to anger
> and abounding in love, and he relents from
> sending calamity.—JOEL 2:13

When I was clinging to my eating disorder, I was so blinded by my own judgmental attitudes that I saw mostly the judging side of God. I stretched it to the point that I sometimes saw him as a brutal policeman whopping people on the backside with his baton. I imitated my inaccurate image of him by judging others and myself harshly.

As I stop judging myself without mercy, I experience God's grace and his deep mercy toward me. I find the compassionate side of him that I've overlooked. When I'm sure he is upset with me, I find that he is slow to anger and is abounding in love. All these discoveries are waking me up to spiritual truths I missed before: God works in me. I don't have to be exhausted and miserable to please him.

*Thank you, God, for waking me up to parts*
*of you I overlooked.*

God's compassion is often underestimated.

# *Fullness Issues*

*You will have plenty to eat, until you are full,
and you will praise the name of the Lord
your God, who has worked wonders for you;
never again will my people be ashamed.*
—JOEL 2:26

Can I trust God to make my stomach feel good
again—to give me a sense of fullness or to relieve it?
If I order a salad for lunch, will I survive? If I scoop
a proper amount of food on my plate, will it satisfy
me? Will it be too little or too much?

Practicing abstinence means following a sensible eating plan and surrendering these emotional eating issues to God. I must trust him to help me eat the
right amount and feel good about it. I must not panic
and grab more or put some back.

If I try to eat normally, God will provide exactly
what I need emotionally.

*Help me feel full but not stuffed
with the right amounts of food.*

A sensible eating plan provides enough.

# *Indifference*

*Woe to you who are complacent. . . . You lie
on beds. . . . You dine on choice lambs. . . .
You strum away on your harps. . . .*
—AMOS 6:1, 4, 5

I never intended to be complacent. At some
level, I cared about others. I felt bad when others hurt.
But I was hurting so much on the inside that I dismissed others who could meet my needs. If being
with someone interfered with my being with food,
that person lost. The drive to feel good was so strong
that I sacrificed the feelings, the self-esteem, and at
times the well-being of those I loved in order to get
my needs met. I was complacent by default. I didn't
have enough time or energy to care.

As I turn away from my obsession, I find moments to pay attention to people I formerly missed.
I find a new energy and excitement for causes I previously felt were hopeless.

*God, forgive my complacency and help me
look beyond myself and my needs.*

I can find joy in being genuinely interested
in others.

# *God Listens*

*In my distress I called to the Lord, and he*
*answered me. From the depths of the grave*
*I called for help, and you listened*
*to my cry.*—JONAH 2:1

Is God listening? Is anyone paying attention to
the mess I've made? These are the questions I used
to ask from the depths of my despair. I asked God to
help me escape, but I didn't think he was listening.

Now I see that he was listening, but that it was
my turn to make a move—to become desperate
enough to give up my obsession with eating, looking
thin, and feeling good. When I called out to God,
he answered me in many forms—support groups,
recovering friends, books written by fellow strugglers
like me.

Throughout my journey, God listens. He hurts
with me and honors my attempts to surrender it all
to him.

*Please, God, continue to hear my cries and*
*help me know that you are answering them*
*even when I don't feel sure.*

Calling out to God is part of my healing.

# *Surprised by God*

*Those who cling to worthless idols forfeit the
grace that could be theirs. But I, with a song
of thanksgiving, will sacrifice to you.*
—JONAH 2:8–9

I pursued recovery because I wanted to change
my uncontrollable eating behaviors. I am surprised
that I am experiencing a spiritual awakening as well.

No matter how much I asked for his help with
my eating disorder, nothing seemed to happen. I felt
as if God had deserted me. I see now that I was
clinging so tightly to my *worthless idol* (my eating disorder) that I missed the ways in which God reached
out to me. He tried to persuade me to surrender
myself to him.

So now when I begin to feel deserted by God,
I don't let too much time pass before I go to him. I
spill out these feelings as well as my desire to renew
our relationship. As a result, I find myself awakening
to God.

*God, thank you for helping me wake up
to you.*

The more I surrender my eating disorder,
the more I discover about God.

# Compulsion-based Relationships

*... if one feeds them, they proclaim "peace";
if he does not, they prepare to wage war
against him.*—MICAH 3:5

Some of my relationships are so closely tied to my eating disorder that they are disintegrating. As long as these people and I practiced our compulsions together and laughed about our disgusting behaviors, we felt close and there was peace. We felt bonded, too, as we practiced our character defects together—gossiping, blaming others, and feeling sorry for ourselves.

Now that my eating behaviors are dying, these relationships are dying, too. The bonds are gone, and I don't know if the relationships will survive. I'm not willing to go back to my compulsive behavior to save them.

I can hope and pray that the relationships find a sounder footing in other common interests, but I am prepared that they may not. This is not the prettiest part of recovery, but it sometimes happens.

*God, I surrender my relationships to you.
Help me discern if any are based
on my eating disorder.*

I can survive the losses of who or what
was entangled in my eating disorder.

# *God Priorities, My Priorities*

*He has showed you, O man, what is good.
And what does the Lord require of you? To
act justly, and to love mercy and to walk
humbly with your God.*—MICAH 6:8

I want to be able to distinguish core issues from peripheral issues. I want to focus on what is important, such as the following.

Justice: I can act justly by being honest about my abstinence and not blaming my problems on others. I can admit my faults and make amends to those I have harmed.

Mercy: I can love mercy by giving myself and others a break. I can reach out to newcomers and strugglers.

Walk with God: I can walk humbly with God by taking time to pray, meditate, and read Scripture. I can surrender each person or circumstance I want to control.

I put time and energy into these priorities and let other peripheral issues take care of themselves.

*God, help me have the same priorities
you have.*

I major in the major issues and minor
in the minor issues.

# Not Down Yet

*Do not gloat over me, my enemy!*
*Though I have fallen, I will rise. Though I sit*
*in darkness, the Lord will be my light.*
—MICAH 7:8

Falling into my old eating patterns sets me back only if I choose to let it. I can fight back and tell my eating disorder not to gloat over me! I may be knocked down, but I'm not knocked out. I may be wandering in the dark, but I'm fumbling for the light switch.

Breaking my pattern of abstinence doesn't mean I'm finished. It means I will start again and continue one day at a time. My slips teach me where my weaknesses are, and I can recognize them sooner. This is a minor setback, not the end of the world.

God is more powerful than the drivenness inside me. His love tells me to get up, brush myself off, and surrender to him all tendencies to beat myself up.

*Thank you, God, for your compassion*
*and kindness when I fall.*

Abstinence may be interrupted,
but it isn't lost.

# *Combat Duty of the Heart*

*An attacker advances against you, Nineveh.*
*Guard the fortress, watch the road, brace*
*yourselves, marshal all your strength!*
—NAHUM 2:1

It takes a while to become savvy about when and where attacks on my recovery occur. I have to watch the road ahead. Holidays are supposed to be fun, but they can be so filled with stress that I want to give up my abstinence. Any kind of transition puts the fear of the unknown in me. When relationships sour for no apparent reason, I feel confused.

During these pitfall moments, I prepare myself by journaling more, keeping with me a list of telephone numbers of people I can talk to, and reading books that remind me of the truths of my recovery. More than ever, I invite God into each event of the day and ask him for the serenity I need to survive. I confess my negative attitudes and my heart hunger as soon as I detect it.

*God, help me recognize my pitfall moments*
*early so I can arm myself.*

Recognizing a slippery place for what
it is is half the battle.

# Writing It Down

*Then the Lord replied, "Write down the revelation and make it plain on tablets. . . ."*—HABAKKUK 2:2

Nothing is so plain as when it's written down. I find out what's behind the traffic in my head when I write down my feelings in a journal. I discover hidden facets of myself when I write a moral inventory. Some of it embarrasses me, but I am proud of my honesty. I can silently write what I cannot say out loud. In putting simple pen marks on the page, I find the clarity I need.

God told Habakkuk to write down the revelation he would give him so it would be plain to Habakkuk and others. By rereading my inventories and my journals, I see plainly how I am changing. I see God's grace at work in me, and I become even more determined because of the incredible struggles I have endured. I return to my world refreshed and confident.

*God, help me find healing as I take an inventory and write in my journal.*

Writing helps me face my feelings and work through them.

# *Deciding Against All Odds*

*Though the fig tree does not bud and there are no grapes on the vines, though the olive crop fails and the fields produce no food . . . yet I will rejoice in the Lord.*
—HABAKKUK 3:17–18

Habakkuk's agrarian culture depended on budless fig trees and grapeless vines for food to survive. Their barrenness meant that some would have little to eat, but Habakkuk made a decision to rejoice in God anyway.

In the same way, I make decisions in spite of the odds against me. At this moment I may want to binge or starve, but I decide not to give in to that drivenness . . . one moment at a time. I feel like complaining, but I decide to call a few people and see how they're doing. I don't feel like going to a meeting, but I decide to go anyway just to help out.

I'm glad for these decisions even if I sometimes grit my teeth and pray, "Lord, help me fake it 'til I make it."

*God, help me make a habit of making these tough pivotal decisions correctly.*

Making healthy decisions is half the battle.

# *Going on the Heights*

*The Sovereign Lord is my strength; he makes
my feet like the feet of a deer, he enables me
to go on the heights.*—HABAKKUK 3:19

In my former busyness, I tried to prove I was a
can-do, worthwhile person. But all that proving of
myself left me empty inside.

Now that I'm giving up on my own strength, abil-
ities, and willpower, I find myself on the heights and
I'm not sure how I got there. The progression of
events is the same:

I consider doing something healthy.

I turn it over to God and ask if it's his will.

If it is, I agree to try it, but I surrender it to him.

The result is that I take risks out on the heights
and find myself miles ahead of where I was. People
congratulate me, and I'm dumbfounded. It has been
a struggle, but God has moved me along.

*God, keep taking me to exciting places
in life I've never been.*

To follow God is to prance on the heights.

# *Totally Loved*

*The Lord your God is with you, he is mighty
to save. He will take great delight in you, he
will quiet you with his love, he will rejoice
over you with singing.*—ZEPHANIAH 3:17

It's nice to know that someone in high places likes me. Someone of importance considers me important.

I can't get enough of hearing that God, the all-powerful one, delights in me. He sees something within me of great value, and he smiles with delight at what he sees.

When I need to be rocked back and forth, he quiets me with his love and sings. Today's verse says he rejoices over the frail, human me with singing! I have his undivided attention, and I am the object of his love.

This focused attention quiets my neediness and gives me hope. I can recover from my compulsive eating. I can know what it means to be valued and loved by others, even by myself.

*Thank you for cherishing me.*

To be loved by God is my highest
compliment.

# The Compulsive Personality

*Give careful thought to your ways. You have
planted much, but have harvested little.
You eat, but never have enough. You drink,
but never have your fill. You put on clothes,
but are not warm. You earn wages, only
to put them in a purse with holes in it.*
—HAGGAI 1:5–6

I never have enough. Whether it's food or clothes or money, I'm always looking for something more: one more taco to eat, one more outfit to wear, one more adult toy to show off. These things will solve everything—or so I think.

I'm giving careful thought to my compulsive ways. I'm tired of planting so much and harvesting so little. I want to fill this vacuum in my heart with something that satisfies my neediness on a continuing basis.

As I surrender this neediness to God, I grow in the sense that he loves me, and I, in turn, am able to see my value, usefulness, and purpose in life. With this in mind, I do without the taco, the outfit, or the adult toy—for today.

*God, I surrender to you all my attempts
to fill my neediness.*

My needs plus the love of God equal enough.

# *Trying Harder Doesn't Work Anymore*

*"Not by might, nor by power, but by my
Spirit," says the Lord almighty.*
—ZECHARIAH 4:6

People have said, "Use a little more willpower!"
I tried following that advice for years, and it worked
for a while. Then my willpower began slipping, and
I felt terrified. Now I feel as if I have no willpower
at all.

That's why the process of surrender rescues me.
Since my compulsion has outlived my willpower, I
see that I will not recover based on my own strength
or the cleverness of some eating plan.

As I let go of my need to be sufficient and show
my willpower, I see how powerful the Spirit of God is.
I don't have to try, strain, or fuss anymore. I can surrender to the one who has the power to do for me
what I cannot do for myself. I am where God wants
me—surrendered.

*God, I acknowledge that my struggle with my
compulsion will not be resolved through
my power, but by your Spirit.*

Trying harder will never be enough.

# Who Am I Doing This For?

*When you fasted and mourned . . .
was it really for me that you fasted?*
—ZECHARIAH 7:5

For whom am I trying to resolve my eating behavior? Am I recovering to please a parent, a spouse, or a would-be spouse? Am I going to all this trouble so people will like me more? Am I hoping to conquer my problems so I can be successful in my career?

The nation of Judah did good things (fasting and mourning) and said these actions were for God; but they were for show. God wanted Judah to do the right things for the right reasons.

If I'm facing my eating disorder to please someone else, it does not work. I cannot abandon this eating behavior, which has been my emotional support, unless I am desperate enough to want to change. I choose to recover because I know it's the best thing for me.

*God, don't let me kid myself about whom
I'm recovering for.*

I can set aside others' wishes and opinions
and follow what I believe to be God's
leading in my recovery.

# *Playfulness Returns*

> *But you who revere my name, the sun of righteousness will rise with healing in its wings. And you will go out and leap like calves released from the stall.*—MALACHI 4:2

As I sense a decrease in the drivenness of my eating, I find new freedom. Much like a calf released from its stall, I feel like kicking up my heels.

I can relax more because life isn't so tense.

I am free to make friends with whomever I like without worrying about whether a person is thinner, cuter, or richer than I.

I can trust my instincts because I'm doing what's best for me instead of what feeds my eating disorder.

I am learning what it means to find serenity.

My feelings of uselessness, self-pity, and selfishness are decreasing.

Finally, I don't fear life so much.

> *Thank you, God, for the many benefits of recovery.*

I am learning not only to abstain from my eating-disorder behavior, but also to participate in life.

# The Tool of Abstinence

*The tempter came to him and said, "If you
are the Son of God, tell these stones to
become bread."*—MATTHEW 4:3

The tempter says similar things to me, such as,
"Because you've been so *good*, have an ice cream
cone between meals (or something else to break your
abstinence)."

Jesus often fasted, which can be an effective spiritual discipline for communing with God. Abstinence becomes something of a spiritual discipline for
me when:

- I surrender to God each suggestion the tempter
  makes;
- I practice abstinence to regain life, not to lose
  weight;
- I am accountable to a supportive sponsor and
  friends; and
- I examine my fear, anger, and self-pity and how
  they affect my eating.

Then I can be content to let stones be simply
stones.

*God, help me understand abstinence
as a spiritual discipline.*

Abstinence is one of several tools
to help me gain a renewed life in God.

# *God's Bread*

*Jesus answered, "It is written, Man does not
live on bread alone, but on every word
that comes from the mouth of God."*
—MATTHEW 4:4

Jesus might have said to me, "Man does not live
on bread [and candy bars] alone..." because he
knows I've tried doing just that.

Now I'm finding nourishment in the words and
wishes of God as well as nutritious food. I need to
read about how God worked with fallible, flawed people in the Bible and helped them achieve his purposes. I need to see how he interacted with these
people so I can see him as the compassionate, yet
demanding God that he is. I need the comfort, reas-
surance, and encouragement I find in God's word. I
need to discover and review healthy principles for
living life. I need to be reminded of my priorities so
I can make wiser choices about my time and energy.

*God, help me recognize my need to
understand your word.*

God's word provides the instruction
and motivation I need.

# *Admitting Powerlessness*

*Blessed are the poor in spirit, for theirs is the kingdom of heaven.*—MATTHEW 5:3

As long as I thought I had spiritual insight, I was impoverished. I thought I could find my way to God by pleasing him and feeling guilty and working harder every day. None of that worked because I was attempting to be spiritual.

My eating disorder helps me see that my own efforts to control my body and to be spiritual are futile. Instead of drawing me closer to God, these efforts drive me away from God.

I'm learning to admit the poverty of my spirit. I am powerless to make myself a spiritual giant; I am powerless to make myself a normal eater; I am powerless to become a content person. I relinquish all these things to God, and I know he will make them come to pass in his time and his way.

*God, I give you my weaknesses and inabilities—I can hardly wait to see what you'll do with them.*

Spiritual paupers have enough sense to keep their eyes on God.

# *God Heals Within and Without*

*Blessed are those who mourn, for they will be comforted. Blessed are the meek, for they will inherit the earth.*—MATTHEW 5:4–5

I have felt depressed much of my life. I have spent hours and days grieving over the damage done to my body. I've let others push me around, even my eating disorder.

Jesus worked with crowds of people who were diseased and paralyzed, suffering severe pain and seizures, and he healed them of their physical infirmities. Then he blessed them and told them they would be comforted in their grief. He told them they didn't have to be pushovers anymore, but that they could be meek, meaning they could have quiet strength.

Jesus does a similar thing with me. He not only heals my body (although in a different fashion), he heals the deep neediness of my soul. He comforts me and gives me quiet strength.

*God, thank you for addressing all my needs—physical, emotional, and spiritual.*

God cares about the the infirmities of my body, emotions, and spirit, and he heals me.

# *Useful in God's Eyes*

> *You are the salt of the earth. . . . You are*
> *the light of the world. . . . Let your light shine*
> *before men, that they may see your good*
> *deeds and praise your Father in heaven.*
> —MATTHEW 5:13–15

Many times I feel worthless. But Christ says that I am salt—a flavorful, restorative substance—and I am light—a source of life for many. He gives me this identity because I have chosen him and nothing changes it.

Jesus tells me that I am salt and light even though I have an eating disorder, I feel incompetent and unloved, and I have hurt others. He works in me to do his will in spite of my defects of character.

My problem is that I don't believe what he says about me. The more I believe him, the more effective he can be through me as salt and light.

> *God, I give you permission to do salt*
> *and light tasks through me.*

I get my identity from who Christ says
I am, not from others.

# *Asking Forgiveness*

*Therefore, if you are offering your gift at the altar and there remember that your brother has something against you, leave your gift there in front of the altar. First go and be reconciled to your brother; then come and offer your gift.*—MATTHEW 5:23–24

I often *need* my eating disorder when I feel twinges of guilt for having treated others badly. My appetite goes crazy when I can't look people in the eye because I've manipulated them or lied about them. I can't practice my abstinence when I know others have suffered for my laziness or impatience.

I can, however, clear away the guilt by asking forgiveness of the people I've wronged and making amends when necessary. As I zero in on my defects of character, God sharpens my conscience so I can see and admit how I have harmed others. He helps me differentiate between my healthy guilt over wrongs I've committed and needless shame over incidents that were not my fault. As I clear my conscience, I can normalize my feelings about food.

*God, give me courage to ask forgiveness of those I've wronged and grace to forgive those who have wronged me.*

To ask forgiveness and to forgive others is to thank God for forgiving me.

# The Less Said the Better

*Simply let your "Yes" be "Yes," and your "No,"
"No"; anything beyond this comes from the
evil one.*—MATTHEW 5:37

Too often I defend myself, make elaborate promises, and give lengthy explanations:

- I said that to you because I thought you thought. . . .
- I promise that I will never overeat again. . . .
- I hope you didn't think that I meant. . . .

I see now that I've excused, promised, and explained to make people like me. But when I offer explanations and promises in such an apologetic way, I am giving others the power that I should be giving to God. I invite others to judge me, and that's not good for anyone.

As I learn to answer to God for what I say, I find that he needs no explanations or promises. God knows my heart.

*God, I acknowledge that you have the power
to be my judge. Help me stop inviting
everyone else to judge me.*

Lengthy explanations and promises are
attempts to justify myself, but God has
already justified me.

# *Pray for Whom?*

*But I tell you: Love your enemies and pray
for those who persecute you, that you may
be sons of your Father in heaven.*
—MATTHEW 5:44–45

Who but God would have thought of *prayer therapy*? I struggle and squirm over trying to forgive those who have wronged me, and it wears me out.

But when I pray for those I resent, it helps me. I pray that God will change their hearts and enemy-like behaviors. I even ask God to benefit their lives. (Sometimes I have to grit my teeth during this part.) I ask God to give them the things I want for myself: enough money to live on, good friends, a job they will enjoy, and a family that gets along. When I pray for these things, my resentments begin to creep away. I understand more of their perspective, and I begin to hope the best for them.

*God, help me pray for good things
for those I resent.*

To pray for others is to care about them.

# When Bad Things Happen

*He causes his sun to rise on the evil and the good, and sends rain on the righteous and unrighteous.*—MATTHEW 5:45

I have let the bad things that happened to me to poison my attitude toward God. Sometimes I've blamed God, thinking that he was picking on me. This distanced me from God, and I've used my eating disorder to survive my rejections, failures, and misfortunes.

Recovery involves accepting reality in every area of life. One piece of that reality is that all humans here on earth experience sunshine and rain. That happier, sweeter life we all hope for will occur in the afterlife, not here.

As I accept this reality, I can make peace with God. Having bad things happen to me does not mean that God is picking on me or that I'm a bad person or that I have no faith. It means that my life is normal.

*God, help me not to take personally the bad things that happen to me.*

Trials and struggles are not attacks from God, but simply dilemmas I need to face.

# *Secret Fun*

> *. . . do not let your left hand know what*
> *your right hand is doing, so that your giving*
> *may be in secret. Then your Father, who sees*
> *what is done in secret, will reward you.*
> —MATTHEW 6:4

Secret good deeds can be fun. No one knows what I've done, and I can laugh in the corner with God. Only he and I know that he used me to do this good thing.

Secret good deeds can also help me forgive. If I'm frustrated with people, it helps me to help them. I may not be able to speak to them in civil tones, but if I button up their kid's jacket, help them put chairs away, or say something nice about them to someone else (taxing my creativity at the moment), I feel better toward them.

This is one form of the spiritual discipline of service. I serve others because Jesus did. Seeing how good it sometimes feels and how it helps me forgive, I see why Jesus recommended it.

> *Thank you, God, that doing a good deed*
> *in secret can drain me of my need to be*
> *admired and my need to resent others.*

To serve is to heal.

# Dejunking Prayer

*When you pray, do not keep on babbling like pagans, for they think they will be heard because of their many words.*—MATTHEW 6:7

When I start babbling a prayer, I stop myself in the middle and say, "What does this mean? Is this what I want to say?"

This is especially true with prayers I pray often, even prayers such as the Lord's Prayer used at the end of support-group meetings. I need to pause before I pray and remember that I'm talking to God, the one who rescued me. I can ask myself the following questions:

- What can I thank him for?
- What needs can I present?
- What faults can I confess?

Rather than being extra work, this little extra effort results in an attentiveness to God that reduces my need to babble at anyone!

*Help me present my true self to you, God, in my prayer.*

In prayer I have the opportunity
to be myself more than any other time
in my life.

# Enjoying This Moment

*Therefore do not worry about tomorrow,*
*for tomorrow will worry about itself.*
*Each day has enough trouble of its own.*
—MATTHEW 6:34

I worry about the future, about what I'll say to someone and what they'll say to me. I worry about the past, about what was said and what I should have said. My tendency to live in the future or the past is a subtle form of escape because it keeps me from doing anything today.

The daily tug of my eating disorder pulls me back to the present moment and reminds me to surrender one hundred percent of my attention to God today. I can stay put and work through today's issues. By the time tomorrow comes, things may change and I'll be better equipped to face them.

What a gift to enjoy today—to be thankful for the love of God and others and to be thankful for what I have and what I'm learning. I can feel more alive and enjoy my days more than ever.

*Thank you, God, for today's moments*
*and for the grace to enjoy them fully.*

I can be content and fully present
in today's activities.

# Judging

*Do not judge, or you too will be judged. For
in the same way you judge others, you will
be judged, and with the measure you use, it
will be measured to you.*—MATTHEW 7:1–2

When I meet someone with abnormal attitudes
toward food or I hear someone in a support group say
something childish, I can back up and take off my
imaginary judge's robe. I don't know the whole story.
I don't know the inner drives and thoughts of that
person.

My role is to give people a break; God's role is to
judge. I may observe characteristics about people, but
I may not condemn or label them. I may pray for
them, but I may not assume that I have diagnosed
their problems. I may share my experience, strength,
and hope when appropriate, but I may not act as
another person's conscience. I'm busy enough re-
awakening my own conscience!

*God, please help me hold my tongue
and halt my thoughts when I judge others.*

The only person I can judge is myself—
and then gently.

# *Perfectionism Denied*

*Take my yoke upon you and learn from me,*
*for I am gentle and humble in heart,*
*and you will find rest for your souls.*
—MATTHEW 11:29

In my perfectionism, I act as if today's verse says, "Take my yoke upon you and groan from me, for I am harsh, and you will find exhaustion for your souls."

Perfectionism is harsh and exacting. There is one way to do anything and it's the most difficult, rigid way. Because I can never live up to this perfectionism, my neediness mushrooms, and I feel I have to squelch it with my compulsion.

To become abstinent and remain that way, I must shed my perfectionism. I do this by openly admitting that I have a large, gaping sore—my eating disorder. That means I'm no longer a candidate for perfection, and I don't have to try so hard. Having admitted that, I can get on with important things in life such as growing in love, joy, and peace—one day at a time.

*Thank you, God, for being so gentle.*
*Help me to be gentle with myself.*

I can allow my eating disorder to remind
me that I am loved and cherished
by God as I am.

# *Considering God's Timing*

*But the Pharisees went out and plotted how
they might kill Jesus. Aware of this, Jesus
withdrew from that place.*
—MATTHEW 12:14–15

My eating disorder taught me to act according to
my feelings and my hunger. Jesus set aside his feelings and made decisions based on God's timing.
Early in his teaching career, he avoided confrontation
so he could have a few years to train the disciples.
Later he confronted the religious leaders, allowing
himself to be killed. This was God's timing for him.

I am learning to act rather than react based on
what I think God's timing is. When I am accused,
I try to determine if it's time to confront or time to
let go. I can trust that there is wisdom beyond emotional reactions and revenge. I may not always understand God's timing or respond to it, but it's important
that I at least consider it, asking myself, "Do I have
peace about doing this now or responding this way at
this time?"

*God, help me try to consider your timing.*

I honor my feelings, but I don't let them
rule my actions.

# *Words*

> *. . . men will have to give account on the day of judgment for every careless word they have spoken. For by your words you will be acquitted, and by your words you will be condemned.*—MATTHEW 12:36–37

Words can hurt. I have to ask myself, Would I make this comment about this person if he or she were standing in front of me? How do people feel about my repeating what they said? Often I choose to make amends for gossip, thoughtless judgments, and words I don't mean.

Behind my words are a *thought life* I have to account for as well. I'm most comfortable around people I love, and too often my unkind thoughts pour forth and hurt them. This thought life is slowly becoming more positive, but in the meantime, I want to check more carefully the words I leave hanging in the air.

I want my words to help instead. I want to use my tone of voice to offer warmth, respect, and even mercy to others.

> *God, please teach me to choose*
> *to speak to myself in a merciful way.*

My words are a practical barometer
of the progress I'm making.

# The Value of Solitude

*After [Jesus] dismissed them, he went
up on a mountainside by himself to pray.*
—MATTHEW 14:23

Jesus frequently went off for extended times of solitude with God. I'm discovering that I also need solitude. I need extended times of prayer, meditation, worship, and Scripture reading to renew me in a way that nothing else does.

Isolation, on the other hand, drains me. I build walls around myself and my eating disorder and I spend a lot of energy refusing invitations, getting out of commitments, hating the thought of doing any work, and fearing that I will lay in bed forever and never get up again.

I'm sometimes so afraid of isolating myself as I have in the past that I fear solitude, too. But I don't let fear of the past keep me from spending time with God.

*God, help me not to fear solitude because
of the way I punished myself with isolation
in the past.*

Time alone with God restores me.

# What's in It for Me?

*Whoever wants to become great among you must be your servant.*—MATTHEW 20:26

As surrendering my neediness dismantles my drivenness for food, it dismantles my quest for power, too. Although I've had pure motives for serving others, I've also enjoyed serving in order to have power over people. In this way, service propped up my flagging self-esteem, but if the service didn't go well, I felt defeated. After all, it didn't impress anyone.

Serving others with only their needs in mind feels empty at first. There's nothing in it for me, and I can't be concerned about myself. It means not letting my bad moods make me ungracious and not caring if anyone appreciates what I do. I serve only because I think this is what God wants to do.

As I get used to this hands-off, selfless attitude, service becomes more enjoyable, which is one more paradox of surrender.

*God, please teach me to enjoy selfless service.*

I can serve because God prompts me to rather than to impress people.

# The Gift of Touch

*A man with leprosy came to him and begged
him on his knees, "If you are willing, you can
make me clean." Filled with compassion,
Jesus reached out his hand and touched
the man.*—MARK 1:40–41

Jesus healed other people without touching
them. Why did he bother to touch this man whose
disease stigmatized him as a social outcast? Perhaps
Jesus was also healing the man's *skin hunger*, his
desire to be touched, as he healed him of leprosy.
Perhaps no one else had touched the man in years.

I, too, have had a skin hunger for healthy touch.
People in support groups have hugged me and even
held me when I've most needed it.

I can offer the gift of touch in appropriate ways
that don't violate others' physical space. Some people
like full-bodied hugs. Others prefer simple pats on
the knee or on the arm. I can't be sure what a person
needs, but I can follow my intuition and offer a healing touch as it seems appropriate.

*God, guide me in using a tender touch
with people who need it.*

Touch can be a powerful nonverbal
message of love.

# Worry over What Others Think

*[The teachers of the law] asked [Jesus']*
*disciples: "Why does he eat with tax*
*collectors and sinners?"*—MARK 2:16

Given the choice between dining out with admired leaders or common sinners, I would choose admired leaders. Jesus didn't. He cared nothing about impressing people. He knew who he was and why he was on earth.

I'm learning who I am and why I'm on earth. I'm a fellow struggler with many other recovering people. I'm not here to impress anyone with a svelte figure or a magnetic personality.

As my self-respect grows, I care less about what people think of whom I see and where I dine and how old my car is. I put my energy into important things like becoming the person God intended, seeking God's purposes in my life, and knowing and loving others.

*God, help me find relief for my flagging*
*self-esteem so I can quit worrying*
*about what others think of me.*

I can replace my concern with what others
think about me with concern for what
God (and eventually I) think about me.

# *Being Freed*

> *This man lived in the tombs, and no one
> could bind him any more, not even with a
> chain. For he had often been chained hand
> and foot, but he tore the chains apart and
> broke the irons on his feet.*—MARK 5:3–4

This man's story is the story of my recovery. The chains I use to restrict my eating disorder (diets) become weaker as the eating disorder advances. The drive to numb out by eating or get high by starving becomes stronger. It resembles the demon-possessed man's life: "Night and day he would cry out and cut himself with stones" (v. 5).

Dabbling with the idea of giving up my eating behaviors is scary. As the demon-possessed man cried: "What do you want with me, Jesus . . . ? Swear to me you won't torture me!" (v. 7)

The one who freed this man frees me. I am not being healed instantly, but it is a miracle, nevertheless, that I can be freed from the craziness raging within me and have the opportunity to discover real life.

> *Thank you, God, for making sanity
> possible for me.*

I can break loose from the chains
of my eating behaviors.

# *Messiah Without a Messiah Complex*

*Then, because so many people were coming and going that they did not even have a chance to eat, [Jesus] said to them, "Come with me by yourselves to a quiet place and get some rest."*—MARK 6:31

How can I go off with my friends when there are so many tasks that need to be done and people who need help? That's my messiah complex talking.

It's interesting that the messiah himself, Jesus, could take a break when he needed it. He even urged his disciples to come away with him to a quiet place.

I'm learning that God doesn't always want me to be a martyr, to do the hardest possible thing, or to be the most miserable I can be. He understands my need for rest, relaxation, and diversion. He wants me to balance my life between my work and my play, between myself and my family, and being with others and being alone with him.

*God, show me what I need to do to balance my life.*

I don't have to be a martyr to be loved by God.

# *Loving Confrontation*

*Jesus looked at him and loved him.*
*"One thing you lack," he said. "Go, sell*
*everything you have and give to the poor,*
*and you will have treasure in heaven.*
*Then come, follow me."*—MARK 10:21

Certain people who talk to me impatiently about getting rid of my compulsion look detached and disgusted with me. When Jesus told this rich man to give up what he was obsessed with, his money, Jesus looked at him and loved him.

God sees me with my arms wrapped around my compulsive behavior and loves me anyway. At times I decide, as the rich young ruler decided, to hang on to my obsession. I may walk away sad as he did, but I remember the love in Jesus' gaze. And when I'm sick of my obsessiveness and ready to change, I remember the love. I know I'm welcome to come back and change my mind. So I do.

And I pray that when it's my turn to offer a similar challenge to others, I can do it with the love Jesus did.

*Thank you for the love you have for me,*
*God, even though I am obsessed at times*
*with my eating behaviors.*

God looks beyond my obsession
and loves me.

# *Rageless Justice*

*Jesus entered the temple area and began
driving out those who were buying and
selling there. He overturned the tables
of the money changers and benches of those
selling doves.*—MARK 11:15

Although Jesus did get angry and frustrated at other times (and anger is not necessarily wrong), the Scripture doesn't say that he was angry in this instance. It's possible that Jesus, with his genuine, caring ways and finely tuned sense of justice, could overturn these tables of extorted money without anger or rage.

As I learn to cope with my emotions, I see that sensing an injustice doesn't have to be an emotionally charged issue. I may feel deeply about the issue, but I can set aside that blaming attitude and present the issue in a fair and reasonable way.

I can stand up for justice without raging on and on. I can be passionate, but fair. Even though I feel determined, I can be sensitive to others.

*When I need to confront others, God, help
me do so in a fair, helpful way.*

I can stand up for justice justly.

# Is Food My God?

*Love the Lord your God with all your heart
and with all your soul and with all your
mind and with all your strength.*
—MARK 12:30

I've separated the parts of my life so much that at times my faith amounted to little more than visiting God weekly at church. In the meantime, my eating disorder filled every moment of the day and took the place of God in my life. I worshiped food and thinness by the way it preoccupied my thoughts and dominated my actions.

As I'm prying the tentacles of my eating disorder off my heart, I have a new hunger for God. I want to love him with my all my heart, soul, mind, strength, and—body! I want to consider him throughout the day. I want to dethrone food and come to know God.

*God, teach me what it means to worship you
in a way that surpasses how I worshiped
food and thinness.*

Whatever I center my life around is what
I worship.

# *Looking Outside Myself*

*The second is this, "Love your neighbor as yourself."*—MARK 12:31

The team approach of recovering from an eating disorder helps me see outside myself. Others also struggle, and I long to connect with them and know them.

Because I feel a team spirit with others in facing my eating disorder, I am more aware of others. I wonder if the person sitting in front of me on the bus, the teenager sitting next to me in the doctor's office, and the executive across the restaurant are struggling, too.

I understand that I can't rescue everyone, but I can give of myself to those God puts in my path. I can pray for them, listen to them, and affirm the progress I see in them. I can offer them the acceptance I'm learning to offer myself.

*God, help me become aware of the people you put in my path.*

Other people's struggles
are as real as mine.

# *Asking for Help*

*He took Peter, James and John along with
him, and he began to be deeply distressed
and troubled. "My soul is overwhelmed with
sorrow to the point of death," he said. "Stay
here and keep watch."*—MARK 14:33–34

I'm afraid I'll bother someone if I ask for help
and that I'm not important enough to matter to anyone. My self-esteem is so fragile that I'm not willing
to ask for prayer and companionship as Jesus did
when he was overwhelmed in the garden of Gethse-
mane. Who am I to need less than Christ himself
needed? Asking others for help is appropriate. It's a
step of growth for me because it requires the courage
to approach others and the humility to admit my
neediness.

*God, give me the courage and humility
to reach out to others when I need help.*

Reaching out for help is a sign of wisdom,
not weakness.

# *Time Alone with God*

*At daybreak Jesus went out to a solitary*
*place.*—LUKE 4:42

The amazing thing about Jesus going out at daybreak into the dew-dampened outdoors is that the
previous day had been an exhausting one (Luke
4:33–41). He had recruited followers, driven out
demons, and healed a lot of people. Why didn't he
sleep in?

It looks as if Jesus slipped off to be with God
the way two parents make time to sit up and talk
after their children go to bed. Jesus, too, carved this
time out of his schedule for fellowship and reflection
with God.

I need quiet moments with God, too. I need to
reflect on the direction my life is taking. I need to
unload the long list of issues that trouble me and
people and causes I care about. These extended
moments set a tone of being aware of God so that in
my normal events of the day I find it more natural to
maintain conscious contact with God.

*God, help me understand how much I need*
*to spend time with you, and help me make*
*it a priority.*

That anxious emptiness inside me is a
signal to spend time with God.

# Respond Instead of React

*If someone strikes you on one cheek, turn to him the other also.*—LUKE 6:29

When someone insults me or picks a fight with me, my natural responses are fight or flight. I strike back with an equally powerful retort or I make an excuse to leave and feel hurt.

There is another choice. I can forgive the person and stick around. I don't stay to get beaten up or verbally abused, but I don't retaliate either. I don't fight and I don't flee.

If my child yells at me, I don't need to yell back. I can give a hug. If neighbors get upset with me, I can continue to treat them with kindness and concern.

I don't respond this way to win back their friendship. I do this because it's right. I imitate Christ. I find that in the process I am not eaten up with resentment and anger, and I don't eat because of what's eating me.

*God, help me learn the gentle art of surprising the resentment out of myself.*

Fire doesn't fight fire; water fights fire.

# *Courtesy and Self-Respect*

*Do to others as you would have them do to you.*—LUKE 6:31

Being polite seems like an unnecessary frill in life, but I'm learning that it's one small sign of respect and self-respect. It's easy to feel I don't have time to be courteous to a sales clerk, a telephone salesperson, or a driver in the next car. Children are often considered unworthy of respect, but my politeness to them shows them that I value them, which builds their self-esteem.

Being polite also means I respect myself and that I'm willing to impart some of my self-respect to others. I can respect others' words, wishes, and feelings. This is one more subtle way to leave behind my self-obsession.

*God, help me reflect your grace in the way I deal with people.*

Courtesy reminds me that God loves each person as a valued human being.

# *Unspoken Messages*

*The good man brings good things out of the good stored up in his heart, and the evil man brings evil things out of the evil stored up in his heart.*—LUKE 6:45

I used to say to myself, At least I didn't say anything; I only thought it. I used to believe that I was progressing if I didn't verbalize the negative thoughts I was thinking. And maybe I was at that time.

But my nonverbal messages can be more powerful than my verbal ones. When I entertain negative thoughts about people, the negative thoughts produce a resentment that makes me quietly ignore or snub them. Then I have to police every thought and every word. This life of hypervigilance is not a healthy one.

I want to expel negative thoughts about others as soon as they appear so I can recover from the inside out.

*God, help me store good things in my heart about others.*

Good words and thoughts decrease the negative traffic in my head.

# Never Enough

*What good is it for a man to gain the whole world, and yet lose or forfeit his very self?*
—LUKE 9:25

In my efforts to feel good about myself, I have not only eaten, dieted, and starved, I have searched for the good life. I have tried to feel acceptable by expending my energies trying to live an upwardly mobile lifestyle, wearing the right clothes, and pursuing a fast track in my job. My neediness forces me to feel I am hopeless without these things.

As I surrender this great neediness, the lure of these things subsides somewhat. Where I live, the clothes I already own, and my present job are good enough. I don't have to prove anything to anyone. God's will is becoming more important, so I spend more time on spiritual growth than on acquiring positions and prestige I don't need.

*I want to love you, God, the blesser, much more than I love your blessings.*

I can pursue God's will and set aside my neediness for money, fame, and power.

# Do the Next Task

*When the disciples James and John saw this,*
*they asked, "Lord, do you want us to call fire*
*down from heaven to destroy them?" But*
*Jesus turned and rebuked them, and they*
*went to another village.*—LUKE 9:54–55

Recovering from an eating disorder can be so
exciting that I get big and bold ideas of what comes
next, as James and John did. I decide I'm going to
abstain from a new food, but I sense God telling me
to simply make my portion smaller that night for dinner. I decide I'm going to start a new support group,
but I sense God telling me to help the one I already
attend.

It's not so much an either-or issue or even that
I must always do the smaller, humble thing. It's that
I can discern what is the next step in my life based on
my responsibilities and limitations, not what sounds
impressive. There may be other times to dream big—
as long as it's God's dream for me.

*God, show me the next thing I should do*
*and help me do it.*

Big ideas are great as long as they are
the right ones for me.

# Busy, Busy

*"Martha, Martha," the Lord answered,
"you are worried and upset about many
things, but only one thing is needed."*
—LUKE 10:41–42

I have *hurry sickness* when I feel pressured to do many things in a short time. When I ask myself who it is that's putting this pressure on me, it's often me. I have given myself goals and deadlines that are unrealistic. I would not be as hard on anyone else as I am on myself.

I'm learning that it's not a crisis if I do something tomorrow instead of today or if I'm late for a meeting. It's true that these imperfections let people know that I'm only human, but that's the truth. I'm not perfect.

When I'm not in such a hurry, I recognize my higher priorities more easily, such as the one thing that Martha needed: to spend time listening to Jesus.

*God, thank you for never being in a hurry
with me. Please help me do the same
with my life.*

I can listen to my priorities even if they
differ from what seems to be most urgent.

# Facing the Drivenness

*When an evil spirit comes out of a man, it goes through arid places seeking rest and does not find it. Then it says, "I will return to the house I left." . . . Then it goes and takes seven other spirits more wicked than itself, and they go in and live there. And the final condition of that man is worse than the first.*—LUKE 11:24, 26

As I become abstinent, my drivenness flares up in new, unexpected temptations and I have to face them. As I quit using food to fill my neediness, I may struggle with spending too much money or fantasizing about the star of the last movie I saw. The drivenness has to go somewhere, and I find damaging ways to process it. I need to face my drivenness and not let it transfer into other compulsions.

I face that drivenness by using my recovery tools such as journaling, praying, meditating, and talking things out with friends. By using these tools, I can do more than stop the eating behaviors; I can work through the neediness behind them.

*God, help me recognize when I'm transferring compulsions instead of facing my drivenness.*

My goal is to work through my neediness to become a whole person.

# *Expecting the Worst*

*Therefore I tell you, do not worry about your
life, what you will eat; or about your body,
what you will wear. . . . Who of you
by worrying can add a single hour
to his life?*—LUKE 12:22, 25

With each financial setback, I see myself out on the streets by tomorrow night. I think that if I expect the worst, I'll feel better when it doesn't happen. Instead I get myself and others upset.

I worry because I have a difficult time trusting God. Most of the things I fear never happen, but I am packed for twenty-seven emergencies and armed with contingency plans.

As I practice one-day-at-a-time living, fear of economic insecurity is leaving me. I don't make things worse by *awfulizing* life. Because I don't worry so much, I am emotionally prepared to meet calamity as it comes. I can be myself and slide through the turmoil more easily. Some would call it serenity.

*God, teach me to view life through the lens
of trusting you.*

Trust can replace worrying and obsessing.

# *Answers in Unexpected Places*

*Make every effort to enter through the
narrow door, because many, I tell you,
will try to enter and will not be able to.*
—LUKE 13:24

The narrow door is surrender; the wide door is control. Others simply join diet clubs and health spas; I need support-group meetings. Why is it so different for me?

Diets and other food- and weight-centered methods only increase the drivenness for a compulsive person like me. Now I stand at the narrow door of surrender, admitting that I'm powerless over my compulsion and that only God (instead of new exercise gadgets or liquid diets) can restore me to sanity.

I see that God often moves in the opposite direction of my culture. In giving up, I win. In surrendering, I overcome. It's OK to be different and swim against the current of my culture when I sense that I'm in God's will for me.

*God, help me to be willing to go against
my culture's love of power and admit
my powerlessness.*

I am taking what may be considered
an unusual route to wholeness, but I
believe it is God's will for me.

# *Love That Risks*

*Suppose one of you has a hundred sheep and loses one of them. Does he not leave the ninety-nine in the open country and go after the lost sheep until he finds it?*—LUKE 15:4

Why would a shepherd abandon ninety-nine sheep in open country with wolves to hunt down one sheep? This goes against logic.

What would make anyone willing to do this? Having what God has: an illogical love for each person; a dogged determination to do whatever it takes to help even one person find him and grow closer to him.

I am that one person, and God has illogically loved me in spite of my faults. He has refused to give up on me even when I've given up on myself and on him many times. This kind of love is a mystery to me, but I thank God for it.

*Thank you, God, for picking me out and loving me, for coming to get me when I've been lost.*

I can accept God's determined, relentless love for me.

# Inconvenience

*Or suppose a woman has ten silver coins
and loses one. Does she not light a lamp,
sweep the house and search carefully until
she finds it?*—LUKE 15:8

What makes a woman look for a virtual needle
in a haystack in the nighttime darkness of her Palestinian hut? Why not wait until morning?

Her methods, like God's methods, are not based
on convenience, but on doing what's important. If I
imitate God in this way, I must set aside my love for
convenience when I pursue recovery.

Going to meetings is not convenient. Listening
to struggling friends is not convenient. Abstinence is
not convenient. But I have set aside the softer, easier,
more convenient way to pursue a way of life that
brings me serenity.

*God, forgive me for my love of convenience,
and teach me to put first things first,
as you do.*

I can imitate God by setting aside that love
of convenience.

# *Talking to Myself*

*When he came to his senses, he said,*
*"How many of my father's hired men have*
*food to spare, and here I am starving to*
*death!"*—LUKE 15:17

Is it strange to plan what I'm going to say to myself? This worked for the prodigal son. After he squandered his wealth in wild living, he talked some sense into his own head.

I can use the same process to contradict my negative thinking with powerful truths about the way life really is. I can even use recovery sayings:

- When I beat myself up: "Progress, not perfection."

- When I try too hard: "Easy does it."

- When I become impatient with myself: "One day at a time."

- When I make a big deal out of things: "Keep it simple."

This is how I can renew my mind day by day.

*God, help me tell myself the truth—*
*again and again.*

Self-talk can be self-renewing.

# *Facing Mistakes*

*The son said to him, "Father, I have sinned
against heaven and against you. I am
no longer worthy to be called your son."*
—LUKE 15:21

My mistakes don't cancel God's love for me. Like the prodigal son, I can always come home, take responsibility for my mistakes, ask for forgiveness, and crawl back into God's lap. I can count on God to restore me.

If I break my abstinence, I can still come to God. Instead of saying, "I'm too ashamed, I can't pray," I can say, "I'm so ashamed, I must pray." Facing up to it is the most healthy thing to do. I can trust God to help me.

I can confess my mistakes to my friends, too. Instead of feeling too ashamed to go back to a support-group meeting because I've broken my abstinence, I can admit that I need to attend and that I wouldn't dare miss it. I know that the others at the meeting are simply flawed persons just like me.

*God, help me trust you and others
to forgive my mistakes.*

The times I choose to run away from God
and from friends are the times I could be
running toward them.

# *Crushed Faith*

*Simon, Simon, Satan has asked to sift you
as wheat. But I have prayed for you,
Simon that your faith may not fail.
And when you have turned back, strengthen
your brothers.*—LUKE 22:31–32

Simon Peter was sifted and crushed when he was tempted to deny Jesus. Jesus prayed for Peter, but it was an odd prayer. He could have prayed that Peter wouldn't be tempted or hurt, but instead he prayed that Peter's faith wouldn't fail.

Peter failed by denying Jesus, but his faith didn't. He didn't give up on God. He later reconciled with Jesus and went on to be a great disciple of Christ.

I have been sifted by my eating disorder. I have felt crushed by it and weary with God and spiritual issues. I have failed, but in a sense, my faith hasn't failed. As I've come to the end of myself, I've realized that no matter how bad it gets, I need God to get through. My faith is strained, but it's surviving.

*Thank you, God, for helping me sustain
at least some faith throughout
my eating disorder.*

My faith in God may grow dim,
but I don't need to let it die.

# *God, My Parent*

> *Yet to all who received him, to those who*
> *believed in his name, he gave the right*
> *to become children of God.*—JOHN 1:12

In addition to my human parents, God is my parent. He fills in the gaps in the human parenting I received. He is there for me no matter what. He does not shame me; he does not even try to control me. He even lets me wander off on occasion, and I have to find my way back.

Because God is my parent, I feel hopeful in spite of my past; God was there watching me, guiding me, and, at times, grieving over my behavior and things that happened to me. I feel hopeful for the present; what happens today is an important part of how God is restoring me. I feel hopeful for the future; God will help me become all that he has for me.

*God, I want to celebrate being your child*
*and knowing you.*

As God's child, I am never without hope.

# *Realistic Expectations*

*. . . many . . . believed in his name.*
*But Jesus would not entrust himself to them,*
*for he knew all men.*—JOHN 2:24

I have depended on people too much. They might have promised with the greatest of intentions to help me but could not follow through. I felt disappointed, bitter, and needy enough to practice my compulsion.

They could not follow through because they were only human. Some were bound up in their own insecurities and they didn't know how to give. Others were caught up in their responsibilities, and they shouldn't have made such promises. Still others had a change of heart and decided to withdraw their attention.

While I have expected unrealistic things from people, Jesus knew that those who believed him to-day may turn on him tomorrow. I need a similar wisdom. I don't want to ask people to give me more than they can deliver. That is only fair.

*God, help me not to anticipate from others*
*more than they are able to give.*

I cannot expect from people the total
commitment I can only find in God.

# *Filled with Purpose*

*"My food," said Jesus, "is to do the will of him
who sent me and to finish his work."*
—JOHN 4:34

When I do something that is meaningful to me,
I can miss a meal and not notice it for a while. I don't
even feel hungry. My hunger is assuaged by the pur-
posefulness I feel when I'm doing something I like. I
may be talking about important things with people or
working on a project that engages me.

When I do things that imitate Christ—loving
God and loving others—I feel fulfilled, and my drivenness nearly dies. It nourishes me, so to speak,
because afterward I feel filled with energy and enthusiasm to do even the tedious tasks of life.

*Thank you, God, for sharing your sense of
purpose with me and for the way it feeds me.*

I find fulfillment in doing what God has
created me to do.

# *Finding God*

*You diligently study the Scriptures because
you think that by them you possess eternal
life. These are the Scriptures that testify
about me, yet you refuse to come to me
to have life.*—JOHN 5:39–40

It's possible to know Scripture and not know the
God of Scripture. It's possible to memorize Scripture
and not have surrendered to God. I can give God portions of my intellect as I read or study, but still hold
back my whole self. Sometimes I may even use Scripture to beat myself up: "If I'm a new creation in
Christ, why don't I act like it?"

Only as I surrender myself to God do I read
Scripture with an understanding of who is talking to
me. Then I am touched by his love for me, his plan
for me, his example for me. Then I am bonded to the
God of Scripture, and I find strength and assurance
for myself.

*God, help me pause before reading your word
and surrender myself to you first.*

A surrendered heart gives me clarity
of vision.

# *Unleashing Food*

*Here is a boy with five small barley loaves
and two small fish, but how far will that
go among so many? . . . Jesus then took
the loaves, gave thanks, and distributed
to those who were seated as much as they
wanted.*—JOHN 6:9, 11

I tend to feel territorial about eating. It would
be a radical thing to give up a candy bar I've saved
for myself. It can sometimes even be difficult not to
care about where I go out to eat with a friend. What
if I have a fixation for a beef sandwich and she wants
a salad instead? What if I'm being *good* and plan-
ning to have a salad, and he wants to go to a greasy-
spoon place?

I'm learning to give up my possessive feelings
toward food and food choices. Food is no longer my
friend or enemy; it is simply a substance provided by
God to nourish me.

As I watch this emotional attachment/disgust
fade, I watch myself find nourishment in my contentment with life. It is not skimpy nourishment either. It
is as much as I truly need.

*Please, God, sever the bonds
I have built with food.*

I can trust God enough to provide
proper nourishment even if it's not what
I had in mind.

# *Climbing Down Off the Pedestal*

*Jesus, knowing that they intended to come and make him king by force, withdrew again to a mountain by himself.*—JOHN 6:15

Because I have tried so hard to please others, they think too highly of me. I've wanted to be honest, but it was difficult to share how broken I was and how I behaved in private with food. While I have liked being on a pedestal, Jesus stayed off it. He knew he was not an earthly king, so he didn't let the crowds treat him like one.

Climbing down from my pedestal means that I share my brokenness instead of letting people think I'm fine all the time. It means that I don't do things just to impress someone. Being transparent about my faults helps me remember that I am only human. And when someone else discovers that I'm not perfect, I don't feel so driven to prove otherwise.

*God, don't let me forget who I am and what I've come through.*

Admitting weaknesses builds strength.

# Judging
# by Appearances

*Stop judging by mere appearances and make
a right judgment.*—JOHN 7:24

People misunderstand recovery—and my experiences as well—when they look only on the surface of things. Shallow thinking leads to inaccurate conclusions:

- All compulsive eaters are overweight. (Many are not overweight, because they also purge, diet compulsively, or simply metabolize food differently.)
- The goal of abstinence is weight loss. (The goal is to stop eating or starving compulsively.)
- The goal of recovery is weight loss. (The goal is to live a surrendered life.)

God asks me to understand recovery at its core. This helps me stop looking at outward appearances in the rest of my life, too.

*God, help me look below the surface at
motives instead of outward appearances.*

I can make accurate conclusions
by considering inner drives.

# *Quick to Judge*

*If any one of you is without sin, let him be the first to throw a stone at her.*—JOHN 8:7

When I am eager to accuse someone, it's usually because I have a problem similar to that person's problem. I get exasperated with someone's negativity because I'm being negative. I am horrified that someone is cheating on his or her spouse because my thought life has not been true to my *significant other.* My own faults not only cloud my judgment, but they also heighten my sensitivity to others who do the same things.

When I judge others for defects of character that I possess, I go back to pretending that I am a flawless, perfect person. I fall short of this every time and drive myself down the road of discouragement. Wholeness involves understanding that others are as bound up as I am and that judging doesn't help them or me.

*When I feel quick to judge, God, help me examine myself and extend mercy to others.*

To show mercy toward others helps me better understand God's mercy toward me.

# *Truth and Freedom*

*If you hold to my teaching, you are really my
disciples. Then you will know the truth, and
the truth will set you free.*—JOHN 8:31–32

As long as I feared that I had an eating disorder
but denied the truth of it, I was not free to recover
from it. Admitting the truth about myself frees me to
do the subsequent footwork: to find support, write an
inventory, and practice abstinence.

Doing these things helps me discover more
truth. Support teaches me the truth that others are
flawed like me, which frees me to quit beating myself
up. Writing an inventory shows me my true defects of
character, which frees me to surrender them. Abstinence shows me how dependent I am on my eating
behaviors, which frees me to admit my powerlessness.

I don't need to fear knowing the truth anymore.
Each time I learn more truth about myself, I can use
it to free myself.

*God, help me not to regard the truth
as an enemy to fear but as a friend
to be thankful for.*

More truth leads to more freedom.

# *Frustrations and Faith*

*Martha said to Jesus, "Lord, if you
had been here, my brother would not have
died."*—JOHN 11:21

I have complained to God as Martha did: "Why
didn't you change that person's mind? Why didn't
you put me in a different situation? Why didn't you
help me?" My complaints arose from my narrow
human perspective compared to God's larger global
perspective.

I begin to make peace with God by asking him
these questions in a direct way, as Martha did. I express my honest frustration and honest faith. I don't
understand immediately, but at least I don't have to
eat my way to numbness just to get through the day.

As if to end on a positive note, Martha added:
"And even now I know that whatever you ask from
God, God will give you." I also try to add some ex-
pressions of faith to my fussing and fuming questions.

*Thank you, God, that I can talk with you
honestly. Help me express my faith, too.*

God values my honest interaction
with him.

# I Need to Cry

*Jesus wept.*—JOHN 11:35

Weeping is one way I *can* imitate Jesus! Since I no longer numb out with food, I experience my feelings intensely and I need to release them. Crying is one way to do that.

Sometimes I withhold tears because I don't have the time to get away by myself, or I'm afraid of being an emotional misfit. But the tears can't be stopped. I break a glass I never liked and find myself sobbing. The tears aren't about the glass, they're about my relative with cancer, my friend who is moving away, and my co-worker who is angry with me.

I'm thankful for tears and how they often force their way through my steely facade. My body heaves and grieves along with my heart. Sometimes, as it happened with Jesus, it lets others know just how much I value them.

*God, please use my tears to create a strong,
sturdy serenity within me.*

Crying is an underrated path to wholeness.

# *Turning It Over*

*Do not let your hearts be troubled.*
*Trust in God; trust also in me.*—JOHN 14:1

Many of my troublesome moments occur because so many things are beyond my control. I can't control my eating behaviors. Just when I think I'm improving, I order too much at a restaurant so I gobble it down or throw it away. I lie about having eaten; either I say I didn't eat so I can eat again, or I say I did so I can starve myself without anyone catching on. My heart is troubled by my deception, and I can't seem to let go.

God tells me in the middle of my troubled moments to turn my hunger and turmoil over to him, so I do. If I take it back, I surrender it again. If I take it back again, I turn it over again by journaling or calling a friend. Gradually I turn it over more easily, a sign that I trust God more easily.

*God, help me do whatever it takes*
*to put my trust in you.*

"Trust in God," is not a cliché;
there are concrete ways to do it.

# In His Name

*You may ask me for anything in my name,
and I will do it.*—JOHN 14:14

I used to plead: "Please make me stop eating, please make me thin, please make me happy." What was missing?

I wasn't willing to do the footwork, I was hoping to use God as a magic wand, especially if I said the magic words, "In Jesus' name, Amen."

Jesus didn't mean for me to use his name as a magic wand. Asking in his name means that I'm seeking to follow God's will. To follow his will, I need to put into practice the things I know are right: release resentments, support others, and practice abstinence. As I maintain conscious contact with God in prayer, I find that he fills my neediness and empowers me to turn my back on food for one more day.

*God, help me follow your will by doing
what I know is right.*

I can trust that God is waiting and willing
to meet my needs.

# More Than Talk

*If you love me, you will obey what I
command. And I will ask the Father, and he
will give you another Counselor to be with
you forever—the Spirit of truth.*—JOHN 14:15

My plateaus in recovery occur when I talk more
than I use the tools. Sometimes I become stuck in
anger and blame, going on and on about what others
have done to me, but I don't work on forgiving and
releasing.

Recovery doesn't work when it's all talk and no
action. I must do a lot of both: talk, especially in support groups; and action, especially prayer, meditation, reading, abstinence, and service.

After Jesus' tough talk about obedience, he offered me some help with my action: the Counselor,
the Spirit of truth will come alongside me and peel
away the layers of my denial. He will guide me so I
can do more than just talk.

*Thank you, God, for the Spirit's help
in putting muscle into my motives.*

Recovery is to be both talked
out and walked out.

# No Fear
# of Abandonment

*I will not leave you as orphans,*
*I will come to you.*—JOHN 14:18

The only person who will never leave me is God. He alone is capable of that kind of commitment to me. Even those who love me very much will die or move away or be drawn away by other important commitments. As orphans are reluctantly abandoned through death, so will I be abandoned by other people.

God will be my only lifelong friend. He is never too busy for me and comes to me when I need him. I don't have to worry about appeasing him or trying not to irritate him. God is the one I can count on to stick with me until death—and beyond.

In the security that God meets my fears of abandonment, I can steady my panic and keep from grabbing food to calm me. There is someone to stick by me, and I have found him.

*Thank you, God, for promising never to leave*
*me and being able to follow through.*

God is the only one who is capable
of relieving my fears of abandonment.

# *God's Peace*

*Peace I leave with you; my peace I give you.*
*I do not give to you as the world gives.*
—JOHN 14:27

The supposed peace my eating disorder gives me is tenuous at best. It is peace by escape, by avoiding trouble, by refusing to face things. When circumstances become overwhelming, the peace crumbles, and my eating disorder cannot put the peace back together again.

God's peace is much more than the absence of trouble. It is a peace of conquest won by surrender. It is independent of outward circumstances. I can go to the doctor and be weighed on the scale and still have it. I can be around troublesome people and still have it. I don't have to go to the convenience store to get more of it. I can use my tools.

*Thank you, God, for this multifaceted,*
*powerful peace.*

True peace is steady and always available.

# *Connected to God*

*I am the vine; you are the branches.*
*If a man remains in me and I in him,*
*he will bear much fruit; apart from me*
*you can do nothing.*—JOHN 15:5

I have tried to have a beautiful body all by my-self. I've spent portions of my life eating grapefruit and cottage cheese, busting the springs of gutbusters, and spending so much money on gyms and weight-loss programs that I could have bought beachfront property (which I would have hated anyway because I'm so anxious about how I look in swimming attire).

My drivenness to tinker with food is a spiritual problem that I can't resolve without the power of God. This drivenness has defined me by what I eat, and I need God to remind me that I am his child. I need his power to push away this eating behavior that is so tightly woven in the fabric of my days—and nights.

I surrender my clever techniques and choose to set up camp in God's shadow and to remain there, one day at a time, forever.

*I admit, God, that I tried everything but*
*surrendering myself to you.*

Dwelling in God is the best place I can be.

# *An Important Friend*

*I no longer call you servants, because a
servant does not know his master's business.
Instead, I have called you friends, for
everything that I learned from my Father
I have made known to you.*—JOHN 15:15

Being God's child makes me feel secure, but being a friend of Christ is a little different. How can someone be Christ's friend?

Understanding Christ's mission on earth positions me as his friend. He came to set me free from my appetite, my fears, and my anger. He and I gather for long talks in prayer, and I begin to sense how much he wants me to recover from this eating disorder and how long he has been waiting for me to do this.

I have quite a group of friends standing around me, cheering for my growth—my sponsor, my support group, and now, even Christ.

*God, I feel honored and loved
to have Christ as my friend.*

I have a friendship with Christ as well
as with others.

# *Rebirth Cycles*

*A woman giving birth to a child has pain
because her time has come; but when her
baby is born she forgets the anguish because
of her joy that a child is born into the
world.*—JOHN 16:21

Nonstop smiling faith isn't real. Life is full of painful moments. But as I work on recovering from my eating disorder, I watch my pain bring forth surrender, abstinence, and even a waning of my character defects. This is anguish.

I can hold on through this pain because I know what's coming. I know the joys of seeing a renewed person come forth. I'm different from my old self, and others can see it. I am regaining a normal body size. I have different eating habits. I have a more relaxed personality.

Because recovery is a lifelong process, these painful rebirths and joyful receptions occur over and over. If they stop, I stop growing.

*God, I give you my grief because I anticipate
the joy that follows.*

Life is full of never-ending cycles
of spiritual rebirths.

# No Concern Too Small

*When [the disciples] landed, they saw a fire of burning coals there with fish on it, and some bread. . . . Jesus said to them, "Come and have breakfast."*—JOHN 21:9, 12

Imagine Jesus, having just come back from the dead, surprising the disciples by cooking their breakfast on the beach. Even in his grand heavenly state, the physical hunger of the disciples concerned him.

Jesus wasn't so lofty and spiritual that he was unconcerned about the physical details of life. He supplied a good breakfast of fish and bread for the disciples. He's concerned with my down-to-earth needs and worries such as cars, computers, and rent payments. Even now he wants me to surrender the most practical or most inconsequential details of my life to him, even the ones I'm sure no one cares about besides me. He enjoys supplying what I need.

*Thank you, God, for being concerned about all my needs.*

God loves my total person and is concerned about my total needs.

# Making the Pure Impure

*The voice spoke to him a second time, "Do not call anything impure that God has made clean."*—ACTS 10:15

The fuzzy thinking of my eating disorder leads me to look at food in peculiar ways. For many years, a potato has been a *bad* food. Actually, a potato is a nutritious food, and it becomes a problem only when I load it with butter and sour cream.

What other good things have I tainted because of my compulsive tendency? Are all support-group meetings *bad* because one was filled with fixing and advice giving? Are all members of the opposite sex *bad* because one of them treated me badly? Are all books *bad* because I have escaped into trashy novels?

I need to shed this extreme thinking that throws the baby out with the bathwater—especially when the baby may be a person, activity, or thing that God has put in my life for my good.

*God, help me respect the wholesome substances and activities you have provided on earth.*

I have access to clear thinking that recognizes unnecessary extremes.

# *Seeking God's Heart*

> . . . [God] testified concerning him: "I have
> found David son of Jesse a man after my
> own heart; he will do everything I want him
> to do."—ACTS 13:22

What does it take to qualify as a person after God's own heart? It has nothing to do with being good enough. David (an Old Testament king) slept with a married woman and then killed her husband.

Being someone after God's own heart is a matter of seeking to do what God wants me to do. What is that?

At least one part of God's will is to shed the bondage of my eating disorder. He wants me to be freed from my preoccupation and guilt. Then I will be free to do the things he intends for me to do. I discover this by inviting him into my daily life over and over, surrendering my fear, anger, and self-pity as I go along.

He will let me know the rest.

> *God, I want what you want.*
> *Help me know what that is.*

To seek God is better than to try
to be good enough.

# Hooked on New Ideas

*(All the Athenians and the foreigners who
lived there spent their time doing nothing
but talking about and listening to the
latest ideas.)*—ACTS 17:21

People wander into support groups hoping to
hear something new. They look disappointed when
no one gives them advice or new insights. Nothing
will be enough until someone waves a magic wand
and takes away their eating disorder.

Hearing new information is not enough. It doesn't
solve my problems unless I do something with it. It's
not the Scripture verses I don't understand that trouble me, it's the ones I do understand and am not willing to put into practice.

Recovery involves work. I talk things out and
make myself accountable. I pray and maintain conscious contact with God. I write inventories and I
journal. I put one foot in front of the other, surrendering each step to God.

*Help me understand, God, that I will not get
better through obtaining new information
but through surrendering myself to you.*

I can push aside that desire for new
insights and do what I need to do today.

# Never Far Away

*God did this so that men would seek him
and perhaps reach out for him and find him,
though he is not far from each one of us.*
—ACTS 17:27

When God seems far away, it's usually because
I've put him there. I've blamed him and even resented
him. I'm thankful he looked away from me. Instead,
he made himself known to me through people and
books, through odd experiences and even the most
ordinary ones.

God stands waiting nearby for me to reach out
for him. He is never content to let me get too far away
from him, even when I try to run away because I don't
like what's happening and I take it out on him. He
allows me freedom to wander, but he reminds me
that I'm wandering away from one who loves and
accepts me.

In time I see that I've separated myself from the
one I need the most, from the only one who can help
me. So I return, and he restores me in his love and
confidence.

*I come to you, God, even when I don't
understand why you allow certain things
in my life.*

God is the one to whom I can turn,
not the one I should blame.

# *Giving Back*
# *Gives Back*

*It is more blessed to give than to receive.*
—ACTS 20:35

When I receive a telephone call from a needy friend, I feel bothered—for the first two minutes. As I listen and connect with what the person is saying, I hear my own struggles and fears being vocalized and I feel better myself.

By then I sit down and I may put my feet up. I relax and become interested in what's going on. I find that the words I say in response are the words I need to hear most. I gain insights I didn't understand before.

When I receive one of these calls, I'm being asked to give. In giving, I receive.

*God, help me to be receptive to the moments*
*I need to give.*

Giving becomes receiving when I have
an empathetic heart.

# A Clear Conscience Feels Good

*So I strive always to keep my conscience clear before God and man.*—ACTS 24:16

It's surprising how good it feels to do good things. A clear conscience begins to feel good, and as soon as I intentionally hurt people or feel jealous of them, I ask their forgiveness and get it off my conscience. It can be embarrassing, but it feels better than a guilty conscience. I like being honest before God.

This clear conscience makes it easier to speak up for myself at appropriate times. I'm not playing that old game, "Well, I didn't deserve the promotion anyway because of the way I treated so-and-so." When I deserve something, I can stand up for myself because I don't have negative baggage attached to the relationships. I feel free and clean.

*Thank you, God, for showing me this new gift of a clear conscience.*

A clear conscience is not only right, it's empowering.

# Unexplainable Hope and Love

*And hope does not disappoint us, because God has poured out his love into our hearts by the Holy Spirit, whom he has given us.*
—ROMANS 5:5

I hobbled into recovery dead inside. My dieting, managing, and fixing had been thrashing me for years, and I felt beaten. It seemed impossible to generate any hope within myself.

Today's verse tells me that it's OK that I feel hopeless and loveless because God is the one who generates an undisappointable hope and a flowing love. As I surrender myself, the Holy Spirit puts hope and love inside me without my realizing it.

There are days when I don't feel the hope and love, but I know they are there. I don't cry as hard and long as I used to. I reach out to others more easily. The gloom and doom is lifting. Yet I know that it's still the Holy Spirit putting this hope and love inside me. They sure aren't my own!

*Thank you, God, for the hope and love you pour into my heart.*

The hope and love God puts within me make me want to continue to renew my mind and shed my compulsions.

# *Just As I Am?*

*But God demonstrates his own love for us
in this: While we were still sinners,
Christ died for us.*—ROMANS 5:8

Most people wait until I show some promise
before they're willing to go out on a limb for me. God
didn't. He sent Christ to die for me even though the
rest of the world viewed me as disordered, damaged
goods.

Yet God scoops me up, disorder and all, and declares me valuable—even before I surrender to him!
He doesn't tap his foot impatiently and wait for me to
be perfect before he loves me. He loves me now—
while I'm still in my disordered state.

When I do surrender, God's love empowers me
to shed my disorder. Much like the princess who
kisses the enchanted frog, God loves me and equips
me to turn into a prince of a person.

*Thank you for loving me, God, when
I haven't cared about you.*

God doesn't wait for me to be good
to go out of his way for me.

# *Confusion*

*I do not understand what I do. For what
I want to do I do not do, but what I hate
I do.*—ROMANS 7:15

I am riddled with behaviors and compulsions
that confuse me. But it doesn't diminish my faith or
progress. The apostle Paul who penned the words in
today's verse was a mature person who loved God
and served him in dynamic ways. This confusion,
then, is part of life. I must never become too proud or
think I'm too *recovered* to admit my struggles.

Being transparent about my struggles is not a
sign of weakness. It shows that I am no longer so
plagued with self-doubt that I can't admit my problems. I keep sharing my struggles in order to get help.
Even though I do things I hate, I am still in recovery
and I am still God's child.

*Help me not to be overcome, God,
by my doubts and fears.*

A certain amount of doubt and fear
is normal.

# *The Exact Nature of My Wrongs*

*I know that nothing good lives in me, that is, in my sinful nature. For I have the desire to do what is good, but I cannot carry it out.*
—ROMANS 7:18

I have tried "trying to be good." I tried to stop thinking about food. I tried to stop being moody and controlling. I kept all this bottled up within me and did my best. Nothing happened, except that I felt worse about myself.

Now I'm doing the opposite. I don't try anymore. I admit to myself, God, and others I trust that I am powerless over food, moodiness, and my desire to control. I no longer pretend to be OK.

I admit this not just once, but over and over, each time I obsess on food, feel moody, and think about controlling. I make it clear that I cannot carry out the good things I want to do. I can do nothing to improve myself. I can let go of my need to appear perfect, and I ask God to take over from there.

*I am not you, God. I don't have the power to work out my own faults. I give them to you to work out.*

I admit the exact nature of my wrongs, and I surrender them to God.

# *Free from Condemnation*

*Therefore, there is now no condemnation for those who are in Christ Jesus.*—ROMANS 8:1

As far as God is concerned, I am free forever from condemnation because I am in Christ. Yet I keep viewing God as a shaming parent who is disgusted with me. I respond to this false image of God by condemning myself, heaping shame on myself, and considering myself useless.

I have wronged God in viewing him as a shaming ogre who is out to get me. Why do I do this? The spiritual enemy tries to convince me that God condemns me so I won't have the courage to think I can recover from my eating disorder.

I have a choice. I can resist these shaming thoughts about God. This is a day-by-day, hour-by-hour task. But it's worth it. I'm renewing my mind and finally finding that I am not condemned and God is not a condemner.

*Help me see you, God, for who you are*
*and wipe away the false images*
*I have put upon you.*

I am free forever from God's
condemnation.

# *Self-Condemnation*

*Who will bring any charge against those
whom God has chosen? It is God who
justifies.*—ROMANS 8:33

Who will bring a charge against me? I will.

I have tried, convicted, and condemned myself. Sure, I know that Christ's death takes care of my sins in his eyes and offers hope and renewal, but I have a hard time believing it.

Now I focus on these truths day by day. When I remember the people I've hurt and the disgusting things I've done, I struggle to give myself a break. When I break my abstinence, I can choose to see clearly that I am loved in spite of the charges I bring against myself. Each day I beat myself up less and agree with God more that there are endless possibilities for me.

*Help me, God, show the same grace
for myself that you show me.*

I am free from even my own charges
against myself.

# Nothing Disqualifies Me

*Who shall separate us from the love of
Christ? Shall trouble or hardship or
persecution or famine or nakedness or danger
or sword?*—ROMANS 8:35

In the past I have let my eating disorder disqualify me as God's child. I figured that God couldn't and wouldn't love someone with a *big* problem.

The truth sinks in slowly. Nothing has been or ever will be powerful enough to separate God from his children—not divorce, not incest, not suicide attempts—nothing. He holds on to me as tightly as ever. Nothing I have done or that's been done to me marks me as an unlovable person. I can be fired from a prestigious job, I can be accused by my friends, I can be disowned by my family. All the things that shock people and make them gossip do not faze God. Nothing makes me unpromotable, undesirable, or unlovable to God.

*God, help me to quit thinking that certain
things separate me from you.*

I can't do anything that would make God
stop loving me.

# *Telling God What to Do*

> For [God] says to Moses, "I will have mercy
> on whom I have mercy, and I will have
> compassion on whom I have compassion."
> —ROMANS 9:15

I've had great ideas over the years of how God could solve my problems. I listed solutions for him: Change my grouchy neighbor's heart; cure my friend of cancer; make my spouse as devoted as the ones described in the how-to books on marriage. Some of these things happened and some of them didn't. I felt that God disappointed me too many times.

I see now that I have been using prayer as a weapon of control. I have tried to control God—as if that were possible!

With a surrendered attitude, I can bring my requests to God in a different way. I'm still fervent and consistent, but I don't have to tell God what to do. Instead, I watch, wait, and cooperate.

*I admit, God, that I have had a power
struggle with you. I will stop trying
to control you.*

To accept God's sovereignty
is one more necessary surrender.

# A Living Sacrifice?

*Therefore, I urge you, brothers, in view of
God's mercy, to offer your bodies as living
sacrifices, holy and pleasing to God—which
is your spiritual worship.*—ROMANS 12:1

Because I'm a living sacrifice, I keep jumping off
the altar. I keep coming up with new get-well-quick
schemes: Maybe if I got this college degree or took
this job or read this book or had a straight-A child, I'd
be OK. Then I have to climb back on the altar and
turn my eating disorder, my self-worth, and my entire
will over to God again.

I'm grateful for God's patience. I'm grateful that
he calls this body I've abused with eating and dieting
"holy and pleasing." He calls my turning it over to
him *spiritual worship.* That sounds pretty holy for an
ordinary person like me. But that's why I turn it over.
God is a power much greater than myself, and he can
restore me to the person he wants me to be.

*God, I turn my body, my will, my mind,
and my emotions over to your care.*

I can trust God to do for me what I have
not been able to do for myself.

# *Mind Renewal*

*Do not conform. any longer to the pattern
of this world, but be transformed by the
renewing of your mind.*—ROMANS 12:2

The people I know and the magazines I read give
me the message that overweight people are ugly and
should do anything they can to become thin. The
more I try to stop eating and dieting, the more I will
hate myself.

I am in need of a major overhaul, a renewal of the
mind. Simply thinking new thoughts is not enough.
I am learning to face my unpleasant feelings and my
incorrect thinking. I can accept God's mercy and stop
judging him. I can view people more realistically and
interact with them more fairly.

My problem actually has little to do with food,
and everything to do with the way I've chosen to
manage the pain in my life. Renewing my emotions,
mind, and spirit prepares me to accept reality and
make better choices in life.

*God, please renew my mind, my emotions,
and my spirit, and teach me a pattern
different from this world.*

An eating disorder is as much about how
I see myself as it is about eating
and not eating.

# *Creating Chaos*

*If it is possible, as far as it depends on you,
live at peace with everyone.*—ROMANS 12:18

Some compulsive people make a habit of creating chaos wherever they go. I am that way. I have been an excitement junkie—a little stab in the back here, a pile of complaints there. I was only comfortable if life was in an uproar. I want to change, yet I don't want to settle for peace at any price either.

Finally, I see the combinations I need. When confrontation is necessary, I can be affirming and gentle. When I have a strong opinion, I don't always have to express it. When things go wrong, I separate what is my responsibility and what is not, and I do my part and wait. I develop the best possible relationships with the people I know, but I accept that these relationships won't be perfect.

In this kind of peace, I find possibilities for genuine positive excitement!

*God, teach me to treasure peace
without worshiping it.*

Peace is usually possible if I clean up
my side of the street and let
the other person clean his.

# *Letting Go of Revenge*

*Do not take revenge, my friends, but leave
room for God's wrath, for it is written:
"It is mine to avenge: I will repay,"
says the Lord.*—ROMANS 12:19

As much as I'd like to think that no one in the
world would wish me intentional harm, I've seen
otherwise. Some people with control or power over
me have taken advantage of me, lied about me, or
tried to manipulate me.

I can work on releasing my desire for revenge as
I trust that God is the author of justice and will
dispense it as he sees fit. I can trust him to be just
and to deliver the consequences in a fair and balanced way.

In the meantime, I can be relieved of the shame
of grudges. I can forgive and go on. I don't need to
knead my anger and fight the temptation to wish
someone the worst. I can let go of it, trusting that God
will dispense justice.

*Help me to trust you, God, to take care
of those who have intentionally wronged me.*

Revenge is no longer as sweet
as surrender to God.

# *Initiative*

*Do not be overcome by evil, but overcome evil with good.*—ROMANS 12:21

If I postpone overcoming evil, it overcomes me. In fact, just about everything I put off seems to overcome me. I think about a task and say I'll do it, but I don't. By the time I finally do it, I've already experienced the agony of it several times.

I am learning the value of initiative. A blossoming compulsive behavior is much easier to deal with in its infancy. It's better to be on top of it than to let it flatten me.

I procrastinate because I'm afraid I'll fail or be rejected. So I gather courage (in case I succeed) and humility (in case I fail) and figure out what the next small step will be. By taking the next small step, minute-by-minute and day-by-day, I become what others call a self-starter.

*Help me not put off the things I need to do today.*

I don't have to do everything today—just the next thing.

# *Bureaucratic Blame Game*

*Everyone must submit himself to the governing authorities, for there is no authority except that which God has established.*—ROMANS 13:1

Even though I'm learning not to blame individuals for my problems, it's easy to blame impersonal bureaucracies. Government officials make mistakes, but I don't need to make them scapegoats. I still have personal responsibilities. My traffic violations are usually my problem, not the fault of law-enforcement officers. Even if corporations and government agencies are careless with natural resources, I can conserve the natural resources within my sphere of influence. I take appropriate civic responsibilities such as voting, praying for officials, and paying the taxes I rightfully owe.

As I clear my conscience and dry up the guilt that my eating disorder has fed on, I can take responsibility for my actions and my resources in every area of life.

*God, help me take responsibility for my own civic responsibilities and avoid blaming officials.*

I can improve my community by starting with myself.

# *Accountable to God First*

*So then, each of us will give an account of himself to God.* —ROMANS 14:12

What's one carrot stick between meals? If it's not part of my abstinence, it's one carrot stick too many.

I have committed my abstinence and my defects of character to God. He understands my idiosyncrasies and why I need to practice the abstinence I've chosen. I don't expect anyone else, except perhaps my sponsor, to understand my eating plan.

As long as I'm rigorously honest with myself, God, and my support group, I don't need to worry about what others think of my abstinence. But I do need to lay it before God on a daily basis so that he (possibly through my sponsor or support group) can help me see what I need to work on.

*Reveal to me the ways I need to change, God, but help me guard against the frivolous comments of others.*

My goal is to hear God's leading above the voices of others.

# Taking Someone Else's Inventory

*Therefore let us stop passing judgment on one another. Instead, make up your mind not to put any stumbling block or obstacle in your brother's way.*—ROMANS 14:13

When I see others violate their abstinence or complain about nit-picky things, what do I do? Do I question them and confront them? Perhaps I do in rare cases, but for the most part I say to myself, "There, but for the grace of God go I."

It's true. I have no right to take anyone else's inventory. I have an eating disorder and I'm surrendering it to God the best I can. I have no time to take another's inventory because I am busy enough using my tools and taking my own inventory.

Besides, when I refrain from judging others, I don't taint my role as their helper. When they are desperate or in need, they know that I am available to help and that I won't bring up negative events from their past.

*Take away my need, God, to tear others apart.*

I am not the judge of my brother and sister, but their fellow struggler.

# *Going the Distance*

*He will keep you strong to the end, so that
you will be blameless on the day of our Lord
Jesus Christ.*—1 CORINTHIANS 1:8

I have excelled in stops and starts. Sometimes
my resolutions to eat properly lasted for a week or a
month. Other times they lasted for a day or an hour.

As I commit my abstinence to God one day at a
time (one minute at a time on rough days), new possibilities open up. I see that with his strength and
help I may stay abstinent for a while, even through
holidays and tough times. And when I do break my
abstinence, it's not the end. Because of God's empowerment in my life, I can call a friend or go to a
meeting and begin my abstinence again.

This is new to me—to think that the paralyzing
cycle of addiction could loosen its grip on me!

*Thank you, God, for showing me the
possibilities of beginning to iron out things
that have plagued me my whole life.*

God's strength lasts for more than just
a moment and beyond the next meal.

# My Body—a Temple?

*Don't you know that you yourselves are God's temple and that God's Spirit lives in you?*
—1 CORINTHIANS 3:16

Contrary to what I have often thought, God considers my body a special item in his kingdom. He calls it—of all things—a temple.

Temples aren't to be worshiped, so I am careful not to worship my body by trying to make it as thin as possible or adorning it with things I can't afford.

But temples are to be maintained because they are places of worship. So I maintain my temple by eating nutritiously, getting enough rest and exercise, getting medical attention as needed. I keep the temple tidy by facing up to and cleaning out feelings of anger and self-pity, as well as self-destructive thoughts. I keep the flame on the altar of the temple well-lit by maintaining conscious contact with God all day long.

*Thank you, God, for considering my body your temple.*

God values our physical as well as our spiritual being.

# Advice They Can Do Without

*For the wisdom of this world is foolishness in God's sight. As it is written, "He catches the wise in their craftiness."*—1 CORINTHIANS 3:19

I can be a compulsive rescuer. I think to myself, If these people would just do what I tell them, they'd be better off.

My amateur therapist attitude turns my thoughts away from my own defects to those of others. Other people's thankful responses to my advice inflate my grandiose impression of myself.

I can't afford to give advice anymore. It deludes others because they relinquish to me their responsibility to get better. It deludes me because I begin to think their behavior and thoughts are within my sphere of control when they aren't.

In reality, I can change no one except myself.

*God, help me to be more careful about rescuing others with advice.*

I want to help others because God leads me to do so, not to feed my ego.

# Slippery Places

*"Everything is permissible for me"—but not
everything is beneficial. "Everything is
permissible for me"—but I will not be
mastered by anything.*—1 CORINTHIANS 6:12

The anything-is-OK-for-me, I-can-do-anything
attitude gets me into trouble. I say that it's OK for me
to eat five potato chips, but I munch through half a
bag and a cup of dip. I agree to participate in a religious fast because someone who is very spiritual but
very unknowledgeable about eating disorders advises
me to. I end up either high on starvation or binging
because I feel so deprived.

If I'm honest with myself, I know the foods and
behaviors that persuade me to slip in my abstinence.
So I name them and I make myself accountable for
them. If I binge at parties, I either skip the next party
or I take three recovering friends with me. These
tools put the breaks on my slips and my I-can-do-
anything attitude.

*Help me, God, recognize and become
accountable for the slippery places in my life.*

I need to make a habit of admitting my
powerlessness, not testing my strength.

# A Body That Honors God

*You are not your own; you were bought at a price. Therefore honor God with your body.*—1 CORINTHIANS 6:19–20

I know that starvation, being overweight, and purging harm my body, so I have a difficult time believing that my body can honor God. Although I can't change what I've done in the past, I can do things differently today. Today, I can:

- surrender my abstinence to God;
- surrender my needy feelings and thoughts to God and process them;
- surrender my defects of character to God;
- make amends to others as needed; and
- maintain conscious contact with God throughout the day.

I will not beat myself up for past mistakes or live in shame. God has forgiven me. I will honor God with my less-than-perfect body by changing my behavior today.

*God, I surrender my abused body to you, knowing that you can restore even the most broken vessels.*

I can't change the past, but I can choose what I will do with my body today.

# *Common Struggles*

*No temptation has seized you except what is common to man.*—1 CORINTHIANS 10:1

From outward appearances, no one struggles as I struggle. No one has the same bulges or eating habits I have. No one feels as lonely as I feel.

When I start thinking this way, I need to be around other struggling people. I need to call a friend or go to a support-group meeting and hear others express the inadequate feelings that have haunted me. I need to hear them admit behaviors as disgusting as mine—yes, they've been sick with the flu, thrown up, and then thought, Oh good, now I can eat again! I need to hear that their hurt runs as deep as my hurt, that they often feel they are alone on this planet with no one standing by them.

When I reach out, I laugh and cry and feel the loneliness in my body melt away. The isolation is gone.

*God, help me reach out to someone like me today.*

In isolation I beat myself up; with support I pull myself up.

# *Keep On Keeping On*

*So, if you think you are standing firm,*
*be careful that you don't fall.*
—1 CORINTHIANS 10:12

It is possible to be vaccinated with recovery—to catch just enough that I never catch the real thing. After a few months of abstinence, I consider relaxing the guidelines for my abstinence. Because I've made progress with my major character defects, I think I am qualified to pontificate.

I can and should celebrate my progress, but I must not forget where I've come from. The behaviors of my eating disorder took many years to develop and they continue to sit in the corner monitoring my success. As soon as I think I've arrived, they are eager to creep forward and say, "If you're so great, how come you're still tempted by your old ways?"

So I stand firm. I look for more subtle character defects and temptations. I use my tools as much as ever. I keep journaling, calling recovering friends, meditating, serving, and practicing abstinence.

*God, help me not to let my pride stand*
*in the way of my growth.*

I use my progress to spur me on
in the adventure of doing God's will.

# Temptations of the Future

*God is faithful; he will not let you be tempted*
*beyond what you can bear.*
—1 CORINTHIANS 10:13

The only way I can survive today is to give up panicking about the future. I give up my annual spring panic about looking decent in swimming attire. I give up my preholiday panic that I'll overdose on sugary goodies or stab one or more cantankerous family members.

I can also avoid panicking about whether God will fail me. Perhaps he's given himself too tough an assignment. Can he actually keep me away from overpowering temptations? For someone as compulsive as I, everything is a temptation.

I can absorb the truth of today's Scripture only if I don't look too far into the future. I can believe that for today God is able to help me remain abstinent.

*Thank you, God, for being faithful today.*
*Help me not to panic about the future.*

Most things I worry about never happen.

# A Way of Escape

*But when you are tempted, he will also provide a way out so that you can stand up under it.*—1 CORINTHIANS 10:13

When God closes a door, he opens a window somewhere. As I learn to trust God, I see that he cares about my abstinence so much that he helps me continue it even when it looks impossible.

Sometimes I don't even look for the open window, the way out he provides. I bury my head so I can't see what's going on. Sometimes I do this intentionally because part of me fights abstinence. Other times I immediately look for the way of escape and take it.

I can't blame my slips on God. The truth is that I'm learning to be willing to take the way out he provides and to even enjoy it.

*God, help me become willing to use the escapes you provide.*

If I look for a way of escape, I'll find it.

# The Nonperfectionistic Abstinence

*So whether you eat or drink or whatever
you do, do it all for the glory of God.*
—1 CORINTHIANS 10:31

Eating for the glory of God? What is that? Is it facing food or the lack of it without any sense of neediness—a perfectly abstinent attitude?

That's a tall order for someone like me. I'm used to appeasing my appetite, even my fixations. If I've gotta have ice cream, I've gotta have it. If I think that Foods A, B, and C make me gain weight, don't even talk about them.

Eating for the glory of God is scary because it sounds so fuzzy. Will a bell go off if I goof? No, and that's the benefit. I can choose an abstinence that I think glorifies God. I may not keep that abstinence perfectly, but now I know that perfectionism doesn't glorify God. Justice and mercy glorify God, and I will abide by my abstinence with that in mind.

*Help me choose an eating plan that
glorifies you and use it with an attitude
that glorifies you.*

An abstinence that glorifies God is born
out of surrender, not perfection.

# *Comfort from God*

> . . . *the God of all comfort, who comforts us*
> *in all our troubles, so that we can comfort*
> *those in any trouble with the comfort*
> *we ourselves have received from God.*
> —2 CORINTHIANS 1:3–4

I used to feel such bitterness toward God that I didn't allow him to comfort me. I was like a child who runs away, hides in her room, and buries her head under a pillow. Then I felt even more bitter toward God because he didn't comfort me.

All that can be over. I can now turn to God and pray and cry in the shower and feel the tears flow with the water down into the drain. I can write in my journal and let the poisonous anger and hurt flow through my hand, into the pen, and onto the pages of my notebook. I can see the painful words lie dormant on the page and know that I have released them.

When I see that others need comfort, I try to listen to them as God patiently listens to me. I allow them to express their emotions, and I remind them that they are loved by God and by me.

*Help me, God, turn to you with my hurts.*

It is easy, but silly, to resist the greatest
comforter of all.

# Healthy Friendship Phobia

*For I wrote you out of great distress and anguish of heart and with many tears, not to grieve you but to let you know the depth of my love for you.*—2 CORINTHIANS 2:4

When I back off from making friends, I think:

- If you knew the real me, you wouldn't like me. You would see my angry outbursts or crying jags and dislike me.
- If I were close to you, you could hurt me. You may ignore me, move away, or become angry with me. Then I'd hurt and overeat or starve to take care of that hurt.
- Being a friend involves work. I'd have to listen and consider your needs over my own. I don't have that much to give.

Before I can develop healthy friendships, I have to believe that someone else will value me. I have to have the emotional resources necessary to rally if that person had to leave me. I have to have crawled outside myself enough to be interested in someone else. I learn these things in recovery.

*God, help me feel good enough about myself to establish healthy friendships.*

My friendships will grow as
my self-esteem improves.

# Invisible Issues

*So we fix our eyes not on what is seen, but on what is unseen. For what is seen is temporary, but what is unseen is eternal.*
—2 CORINTHIANS 4:18

I have focused on something I can see and measure to sustain me—too much food, too little food. I have measured myself against others—Am I the right weight? Is she thinner? Is he more overweight? Am I more attractive? I have weighed and measured my way through too many diets. These actions don't work in the long run.

Now I focus more on the unseen. I see that my eating disorder has spiritual dimensions and that I can examine the way I view God and how I think he sees me. I must figure out just whom I really depend on and why. As I work through these issues and surrender myself to God, I'm better equipped to eat sensibly and work through my psychological problems.

*God, help me see that my eating disorder is riddled with spiritual issues.*

Fixing my thoughts on what is unseen
helps me maintain a proper perspective.

# New-Found Freedom

*Therefore, if anyone is in Christ, he is a new creation; the old has gone, the new has come!*—2 CORINTHIANS 5:17

Even though I have felt completely bound up in my eating disorder, I know that Christ has freed me to become a new creation. The essential battle has been fought, and I have been claimed as God's child.

The possibilities for me are endless. I have the freedom to choose to follow God's will in my life rather than the cycle of compulsive behavior: pre-occupation, ritualization, compulsive behavior, and despair (for more explanation, see glossary). I am not absolutely bound up.

My responsibility is to walk in this freedom and grow. As I do so, spiritual reality becomes physical reality.

*Thank you, God, for making me a new creation in you. Help me walk in that freedom.*

I am freed as a new creation, and with God's help, I can grow in that freedom.

# *God's Co-worker*

*As God's fellow workers we urge you
not to receive God's grace in vain.*
—2 CORINTHIANS 6:1

I am a co-worker of God because he and I work together now. I am surrendering my appetite, my drivenness, and my body image to God, and together we are working out my struggles. Together we are concerned about my growth.

As God's co-worker, I become concerned, as God is, about others' struggles and growth. I ask him how he wants me as his partner to help others grow. I make myself available as needed.

I see God's mission here on earth—to bring us together with him so we may know him and love him. I don't want this understanding to be in vain. I want to help others reconcile to him as opportunities arise.

*I enjoy cooperating with you. Help me
follow your directions—and forgive me
when I don't.*

God commissions compulsion-riddled
humans such as me to partner with him
in his work.

# When Sorrow Is Good

*Godly sorrow brings repentance that leads to
salvation and leaves no regret, but worldly
sorrow brings death.*—2 CORINTHIANS 7:10

Worldly sorrow brings death because it is filled
with shame, despair, and regret. There's no relief from
this sorrow, so I practice my eating disorder. That
leads to more shame, despair, and regret. Depression
chases me from corner to corner.

When sorrow is godly, God's grace is mixed in it.
I know that God pardons me and gives me what I
need to start over. This grace allows me to examine
my defects of character without beating myself up.

Godly sorrow turns me around. I reject my self-
obsession and consider serving others. My inner rest-
lessness tells me to seek God's presence and talk with
him longer than usual. My deepest and finest decisions are made in moments of godly sorrow.

*Thank you, God, for my godly sorrow
and for speaking to me through it.*

Godly sorrow brings turning points
in my life.

# Stop, Look, and Listen Inventories

*. . . we take captive every thought and make it obedient to Christ.*—2 CORINTHIANS 10:5

I'm installing a symbolic trapdoor at the top of my skull. As a thought comes whizzing into my mind, I open the door, take the thought out, and examine it to see if it is healthy, reasonable, and godly. If so, I put it back in and let it do its work.

If not, I face it. I don't gag this captive thought and deny its existence. I treat it with respect. I listen to the feelings behind it. I may have to talk about it with someone else. I don't let go of it until I face it.

This type of intervention helps. I try to pray for my enemies before they become enemies and hand over resentments before they bloom into grudges. These stop-look-and-listen inventories save me anxiety later.

*Teach me to face and process my negative thoughts.*

Intercepting a negative thought works better than curing it.

# *Comparisons and Competition*

*We do not dare to classify or compare
ourselves with some who commend
themselves. When they measure themselves
by themselves and compare themselves
with themselves, they are not wise.*
—2 CORINTHIANS 10:12

Her thighs are bigger than mine. He eats three
times as much as I eat. My face is more attractive than
hers. He gets more laughs when he shares in the support group than I do. Comparing makes for craziness.

If I'm honest, each of my comparisons is a self-
esteem check. Am I OK today based on how I stack
up against someone else? Or do I feel good about
myself only if the other person looks worse?

I'm learning that I can be loved as I am, and I
don't have to compete anymore. I measure myself
against my own goals. I see my progress, I see my
defects, and I set my face toward that maturity. I avoid
becoming sidetracked by comparisons.

*I look to you, God, for the measure of who
I can be, not to others.*

I'm needy when I compare. It's time
to check my feelings and take
a quick inventory.

# *Being Exploited Is Not Saintly*

*In fact, you even put up with anyone who enslaves you or exploits you or takes advantage of you or pushes himself forward or slaps you in the face.*—2 CORINTHIANS 11:20

Some have mistakenly said that the Christian thing to do is to be pushed around, exploited, and taken advantage of. The apostle Paul said this wasn't true.

I'm glad Paul said that because being victimized makes me feel needy, which inflames my eating disorder. I have to numb out so I don't hear the healthy drives inside me that say:

- You don't have to be loyal to people who don't merit loyalty.
- You don't have to try to please people at your own expense.
- You don't have to be abused physically or emotionally.

I have decided to stop placing myself in situations in which I am pushed and exploited. I take care of myself so I don't feel so demeaned that I have to eat.

*God, help me change my course when I see an unhealthy situation develop.*

To respect myself and ask that others respect me is not an un–Christian attitude.

# When Weakness Is Strength

> . . . I was given a thorn in my flesh, a messenger of Satan, to torment me. Three times I pleaded with the Lord to take it away from me. But he said to me, "My grace is sufficient for you, for my power is made perfect in weakness. . . . For when I am weak, then I am strong.—2 CORINTHIANS 12:7–10

"Haven't you taken care of that eating disorder yet?" others ask me. I even ask myself this question.

My eating disorder is my "thorn in the flesh." It is my lifetime reminder that God's grace is enough. It reminds me that when I am weak, God makes me strong.

My eating disorder is my insurance policy that I will never again think I can do it all myself, that I will not fall into the trap of self-sufficiency, and that I will not forget whose person I truly am and whose grace saves me.

The thorn still hurts, but I can live with it.

*God, thank you (I think) for this "thorn in the flesh." Help me put it to good use.*

I live with a constant reminder to lean on God at all times.

# A Servant, Not a Star

*If I were still trying to please men, I would not be a servant of Christ.* —GALATIANS 1:10

When I served in the past, did I do it to earn points with God? to be admired by others? to feel better about myself? to feel worthwhile? Or was it a combination of these motives?

Now I know I live to please God first, not to impress others. When I want to be a star, I ask myself: Why am I doing this? Does it matter who knows I'm doing this? If it fails, will my self-worth be affected?

When I serve only because I'm a servant of Christ, I'm free to serve without building resentment. I don't burn out so quickly because I'm doing it for God and in his strength, not to feel better about myself. I use the gifts he's given me to fulfill purposes he's given. It's all in his hands.

*Help me, God, serve others without self-consciousness.*

As I become less self-obsessed,
my freedom to serve increases.

# *Rigidity*

*There is neither Jew nor Greek, slave nor free, male nor female, for you are all one in Christ Jesus.*—GALATIANS 3:28

Today's verse challenged its first-century readers to change their way of thinking and view people beyond the rigid categories of their culture. In the same way, recovering from an eating disorder challenges my rigid categories, my harsh viewpoints, and my prejudicial ruts. I don't identify people so much by how they are different from me but by what we have in common. I identify with the drivenness of the alcoholic. I see that Christians who approach their faith differently than I do may have something to teach me. I see that people throughout the world with very different customs and cultures want what I want: freedom to make a living and to be with those they love.

The result is that I'm less suspicious of others and more open to God's will.

*God, save me from my former rigidity and help me to be absolute about only those things that are absolute.*

A rut is a grave with the ends kicked out.

# *Choking on Legalism*

*It is for freedom that Christ has set us free.
Stand firm, then, and do not let yourselves be
burdened again by a yoke of slavery.*
—GALATIANS 5:1

Because I am good at making myself feel guilty,
I am prone to legalism. When I hear others say they
are giving up chocolate, I feel I should do the same
thing. When I hear that others have written their
inventory in a certain way, I feel I should do it that
way to be right.

God doesn't send down a carton of size-five
jumpsuits and say, "Anyone who can fit into these is
OK." God is not a robot, and he doesn't ask me to be
one either. I am free to expand my relationship with
him by asking him to show me the weight, abstinence, and sponsor I need. Sure, I may hear him
incorrectly, but he accepts that I'm human and prone
to mistakes. He gives me the freedom to make these
mistakes and correct them.

*God, show me the weight, abstinence, and
sponsor that are most healthy for me.*

I am no longer in bondage to diets
and weight charts.

# *Restoring Others*

*Brothers, if someone is caught in a sin, you who are spiritual should restore him gently. But watch yourself, or you also may be tempted.*—GALATIANS 6:1

Confrontation doesn't work unless I set aside my grandiose know-it-all attitudes. I can no longer play armchair psychologist and diagnose every possible eating-disordered person in town.

My goal and hope is to see people restored to wholeness. I don't come with answers, I come with questions. I don't come with solutions, I come with experience, strength, and hope. I don't come with plans, I come with possibilities. I lay these before my friend and let the friend take responsibility for her own behavior. I am simply one beggar telling another beggar where to find bread.

I also know that as I say this to my friend, I'm bound to face the same problem the next day.

*God, give me courage to confront as needed, but help me do so with gentleness and the same mercy toward others you show me.*

Not decimation, but restoration.

# *Burdens Are for Sharing*

*Carry each other's burdens, and in this way you will fulfill the law of Christ.*
—GALATIANS 6:2

With my old attitude I would say, "That person sure is messed up!" With my new attitude I say, "That person sure is bound up."

It's a new thought to carry others' burdens instead of attacking them for their burdens. Instead of playing against them on an opposing team, I am trying to play on their team to see how I can help.

But how much can I help? God does the unbinding. I can listen, even at odd hours. I can invite them to come along with me at times. I can share my experiences so they know they are not alone. I can pray for them in their struggles. I can watch their burden be cut in half just by sharing it—and the joy doubled as they share that, too.

*Teach me, God, to see others' burdens as something I can help them carry, instead of reasons to attack them.*

My role is not to increase burdens, but to help carry them.

# *Magical Thinking*

*Do not be deceived: God cannot be mocked.*
*A man reaps what he sows.*—GALATIANS 6:7

I have deceived myself in the past by believing in magical weight-control cures. I thought one more exercise gadget, quick liquid diet, or mind-control tape would do the trick. I have also deceived myself into thinking that eating junk food won't harm me. I've thought one more candy bar or bag of chips wouldn't make a difference.

I must ignore the magical thinking of my culture. Being thin doesn't solve problems, and pounds don't melt away! Part of recovery is accepting reality. Quick and easy solutions don't work because I have a physical, psychological, and spiritual problem. The only way to maintain proper weight is through a balanced diet and proper exercise. My body suffers when I eat a lot of junk food, no matter how *lite* or unsalted it may be. That's reality.

*God, help me face the realities*
*of metabolizing food and maintaining*
*proper weight.*

God does not bend physiological
principles just because advertisers show
pencil-thin people munching out.

# *Burnout Blues*

*Let us not be weary in doing good, for at the proper time we will reap a harvest if we do not give up.*—GALATIANS 6:9

I cringe to think of how I've strained and forced myself into rigid diets and exercise plans. I've spent a lot of time subtly pushing other people to do things. I've even told God what to do and when and where things should happen. All that straining and coercing doesn't work. When I give myself, others, and even God deadlines and nobody meets them, I become upset and burn out.

My effectiveness does not depend on how fast others do what I think they should do. What I think would be best may not even be best at all. When I lean on God's timing and trust him to do things in his perfect time, I don't become so weary. It's another surrender—my timing and my methods for God's timing and God's methods.

*God, help me stand by patiently as you do things in your time.*

Weariness is a sign that I'm taking
on God's role, and I need to give it up.

# Accepting
# My Personality

*For we are God's workmanship, created
in Christ Jesus to do good works, which
God prepared in advance for us to do.*
—EPHESIANS 2:10

My personality is different from the one I imagine the ideal person to have. Even though I make progress, I see that I have innate personality traits that seem to handicap me: I'm too high-strung. I'm not smart enough. I'm too shy. I'm too dull. I'm not a leader. I feel miles behind others.

Yet I recognize this attitude as more of the perfectionistic, magical thinking from the past. I am God's workmanship—even my personality. Like a tailor who creates a new garment, God created me with great care. Yes, I'm a little different from the rest, but that's OK. God urges me to continue to work on my defects of character, but not to be afraid to fulfill my purposes using the personality he has given me.

*God, help me see the advantages of
my personality and continue to work on my
defects of character.*

I accept the personality God gave me
and let him work within it.

# Self-Confidence

*In [Christ] and through faith in him we may
approach God with freedom and
confidence.*—EPHESIANS 3:12

At times my still-warped view of God makes me
see myself groveling, terrified, and shamed standing
before him. Approaching God with freedom and confidence is a new idea. I'm free to express myself, and
I'm confident that he loves me.

This image of me as a free, confident person
standing before God gives me self-respect. I see that
God respects me, and I'm more able to quit shaming
myself. I see that the person in the mirror is not a fat
cow but a child of God. I see that I was not created to
be talked down to; I can speak up for myself. I see that
I don't have to push and punish myself; I can relax
and enjoy times of leisure, too.

Since God respects me, who am I to do less?

*Thank you, God, for respecting me and
encouraging me to feel free and confident.*

My confidence comes from God's
view of me.

# *Gentleness and Patience*

*Be completely humble and gentle; be patient,
bearing with one another in love.*
—EPHESIANS 4:2

As I learn to be gentle with myself—to give myself time to rest and room to make mistakes—I can be more gentle with others, too. The more mercy I give myself, the more mercy I feel toward my children, my support-group members, and those I help. I can expect that people will make mistakes instead of being appalled by them.

When I become demanding, I can shift gears and slow down. When I question someone's motives, I can give them the benefit of the doubt. Like a gentle parent, I can confront others when necessary, but I don't do it because I feel impatient with them.

I can set aside my own drives and feelings for a minute to consider the other person. What a miracle!

*God, help me grow in gentleness with others.*

Gentleness helps me get along with others
and myself.

# A Daily Choice

*You were taught, with regard to your former
way of life, to put off your old self, which is
being corrupted by its deceitful desires; to be
made new in the attitude of your minds;
and to put on the new self, created to be like
God in true righteousness and holiness.*
—EPHESIANS 4:22–24

I can't simply fix my old self, so God offers me
a new self. Having a new self doesn't mean I erase the
hurts of my past, but I can be free of their hold on me
and work through them.

Each day, each hour, each moment, I choose
whether to resort to my old self or put on the new
one. As the pain of my past presents itself in my
mind, I can choose to acknowledge that former pain,
forgive and make amends, and release it. Or I can
choose to act on that pain with my eating disorder.

Each little choice enhances or diminishes my
overall choice to recover.

*When I feel discouraged, God, remind me
that you give me choices to reject
my compulsiveness.*

Today's choices bring new opportunities,
and I see that life is not hopeless.

# Lying

*Therefore each of you must put off falsehood
and speak truthfully to his neighbor, for we
are all members of one body.*
—EPHESIANS 4:25

Lying seems like such an ugly thing—how can
I admit to this? On the other hand, lying and deceit
are a large part of an eating disorder. I've made it look
as if I didn't eat when I did or that I did eat when I
didn't. I've exaggerated when reporting my weight
gains and losses. I've lied about how much I ate and
I've claimed to have eaten only broccoli when I also
downed half a bag of corn chips. I've lied to cover up
my mistakes, and I've exaggerated my problems to get
sympathy.

I can tell the truth now because I'm not so afraid
of the flawed person that I am. Others with eating disorders appreciate my honesty and even laugh at my
distorted actions. Because of their love, I can present
myself truthfully to others as well.

*God, lift my shame, and enable me
to tell the truth.*

I don't have to lie because I am accepted
as I am.

# *Anger Can Work for Me*

*In your anger do not sin: Do not let the sun
go down while you are still angry,
and do not give the devil a foothold.*
—EPHESIANS 4:26–27

My anger itself is not bad; it's what I do with my anger that matters. If it gains a foothold on me, it can become destructive. If I nurse it, it will haunt me, make me hold grudges, and fester into hurtful comments. If I try to bury my anger, it will sour within me and turn into depression.

Anger can work for me or against me. I can face it by journaling my angry words, praying angry prayers, talking through my anger with my sponsor or support group, or even pouring my excess anger into playing music or sports. I don't have to let my anger control me.

This process also helps me see how I can use my anger for good. My righteous indignation can get me out of the chair and moving to do things I need to do but have not had the courage to do.

*Help me face my anger, God, before it
becomes destructive and use it to motivate
myself to do things I've been putting off.*

I can choose to make anger a positive
force in my life.

# *Believing in God's Plans for Me*

*Being confident of this, that he who began
a good work in you will carry it on
to completion until the day of Christ Jesus.*
—PHILIPPIANS 1:6

When something good happens, I doubt myself. This is a fluke—I'll goof up tomorrow, I think. So I become nervous, and the first time I fall short of perfection I chide myself.

I can do the opposite. I can encourage myself and cheer myself on. This is not a false, sugar-coated approach to life. I have a promise from God that he will complete the good works he has begun within me. God is as concerned about my progress as I am, even more. Outward circumstances may worsen, but God's work continues.

So I don't get down if my abstinence gets sloppy or I lose my temper with a difficult person. I start over and go on. I am confident that good things are not in the past, but in the present and the future.

*Thank you, God, for believing in me much
more than I believe in myself.*

God will continue the good work
he has begun in me.

# *Interested in Others*

*Each of you should look not only to your
own interests, but also to the interests of
others.*—PHILIPPIANS 2:4

As I lose my desperate self-absorption, I find that
I'm genuinely interested in others and their welfare.
As I let go of my self-pity, I feel the pain of others
struggles, and I see them with a more caring perspective. As I learn to feel the feelings I've masked, I'm not
so afraid of intimate friendships. And paradoxically,
as I share my own neediness, I respect others more
because I'm not feeling superior to them for being
one who always gives but never receives.

Being interested in others nourishes the spiritual
qualities I've prayed for: love, patience, kindness, and
gentleness. That's how spiritual growth works. God
transforms me when I'm not even aware of it.

*God, give me a heart for others, and help me
care for them in healthy ways.*

Serenity involves acknowledging the value
of each person.

# *Self-Pity*

*Do everything without complaining or arguing.*—PHILIPPIANS 2:14

My self-pity manifests itself in the form of complaining. I don't like the way I'm treated, I don't like the people in charge, I don't like the weather. Sometimes I gripe directly to God: Why is he letting me down? Why can't I have a taste of success? Why is life so unfair?

Sitting in support groups helps me see that I feel sorry for myself because of my narrow perspective. As I listen objectively to others, I see that I often block out logic. That person didn't slight me—she just didn't see me. The people in charge have struggles beyond what I can imagine. I don't like the rain, but the earth needs it.

When I crawl out of my little world and see people and situations more objectively, I don't feel sorry for myself.

*God, teach me to see life more objectively,*
*not from my own narrow point of view.*

I can crawl outside myself and see life
from a more logical perspective.

# *Eager to Keep Going*

*Not that I have already obtained all this, or have already been made perfect, but I press on to take hold of that for which Christ Jesus took hold of me.*—PHILIPPIANS 3:12

By rereading my journals or bumping into a long-ago acquaintance, it becomes obvious that I'm becoming a different person.

I get excited about the idea of becoming truly abstinent from the heart—not even noticing the aroma of a nearby bakery, not flinching in the least when I pass a mirror. Could I ever have the serenity I see in people who have been abstinent for a long time?

So I press on, and on, and on, one day at a time, quietly doing the footwork that needs to be done today. The more I press on, the more I understand life and the more I see the purposes for which Christ Jesus took hold of me.

*God, thank you for how far you've brought me and for how far you're going to take me.*

As my obsession slowly fades, I become more excited about what God has in store for me.

# *Living in the Past*

> *. . . one thing I do: Forgetting what is behind and straining toward what is ahead, I press on toward the goal to win the prize for which God has called me. . . .* —PHILIPPIANS 3:13–14

There are many reasons for regret: the people I hurt, the opportunities I missed, the unrepairable abuse I did to my body. If I live in regret, I'll beat myself up, which pushes me further behind.

I can choose instead to make amends and restitution. I can choose to admit my humanity—yes, I made many, many mistakes. I can choose to discover my character defects and surrender them to God to be turned into strengths.

Even when I consider the most unforgivable things I've done, I remember that today's verse was written by Paul, a former mass murderer turned apostle.

Who am I not to forgive myself when God is so forgiving?

*Forgive me, God, for the mistakes of my past and help me use them to live today.*

I can't change my past, but I can move far beyond it.

# *Back to Basics*

*Do not be anxious about anything,
but in everything, by prayer and petition,
with thanksgiving, present your requests
to God.*—PHILIPPIANS 4:6

I clench my teeth when someone tosses off the cliché, "Pray about it." It's a cliché in the sense that many people say it, but it's not trite or simple. When I stop to pray about something, it forces me to sort things out in God's presence, and I often see a new slant on it. I see ways I've been wrong or new possibilities that haven't occurred to me before.

Sometimes I forget to bring the simplest things before God: choosing or refining my abstinence, facing a potluck dinner, eating out with friends. But when I do, God answers in his time. Someone I trust makes a helpful suggestion, or God helps me remember comments people have made. Sometimes I sense that he is slowing me down to get me in sync with his timing.

*Lord, make your ways and timing
plain to me.*

God is big enough to be concerned
about little things.

# Negative Thinking

*Finally, brothers, whatever is true, whatever is noble, whatever is right, whatever is pure, whatever is lovely, whatever is admirable—if anything is excellent or praiseworthy—think about such things.*—PHILIPPIANS 4:8

I didn't call it distrust, I called it facing reality. I figured that anything that could go wrong would go wrong, but I didn't espouse it as cheerfully as those who quote Murphy's Law do. I had a me-against-the-world attitude, and I figured that if someone could get mad at me they probably would. I lived in fear that my house could burn down or my child could die tomorrow.

Now I see that these crises are possibilities, but I refuse to worry about them. I can assume the best and even be right at times. I enjoy life more because I see the good in others and appreciate it. Someday soon I hope to be one of those interesting people who always finds good in unexpected people and places.

*God, help me shed my cynical ways and focus on the many positive things you've done on this earth.*

Trusting means choosing to be optimistic until I'm given reasonable evidence to think otherwise.

# *Overachievers*

*I can do everything through him who gives
me strength.*—PHILIPPIANS 4:13

I used to think this verse meant I *could* do everything so I *should* do everything. I accepted positions
I didn't like or feel compatible with because I thought
God loved superachievers. Besides, it made me feel so
worthwhile to "do it all."

Now I see that doing everything means that I
wait for God to define just what *everything* may be. If
I don't want to do something, I explain this to God
and wait for him to change my mind. If he doesn't,
I don't do it. I trust that God will not browbeat me
into working at things I hate, but that he will work
through me and in me, giving me not only strength,
but also appropriate conviction and desire.

*Thank you, God, for the strength you provide
to help me do everything I should do,
for today.*

God provides strength for the tasks
I need to do.

# Giving Back
# Without Fixing

*My purpose is that they may be encouraged
in heart and united in love, so that they may
have the full riches of complete
understanding.*—COLOSSIANS 2:2

One way to *fix* people is to help them but limit
them in some way by crossing their boundaries.
Because I feel grandiose, I think they must follow my
advice to live correctly. Because I feel entangled, I feel
their failure or success reflects on me. Because I feel
controlling, I will be disappointed if they don't copy
me or follow my advice.

I'm learning to help others, but to let them make
their own choices. They don't have to do things my
way. When I function this way as a friend, parent,
spouse, sponsor, or partner in a project, I feel content.
I am fulfilling one of my purposes in life—to assist
others in finding maturity and recovery, knowing that
their growth doesn't depend on me but on God and
their own choices.

*God, teach me to love people and help them
with no strings attached.*

To truly help others is to equip them to
help themselves.

# My Hiding Place

*For you died, and your life is now hidden
with Christ in God.*—COLOSSIANS 3:3

As I gradually surrender more and more of myself to God, my desires become more aligned with
his. It feels to me as if our identities have blended, as
if there's an indistinct line where I stop and God
begins. (This line is probably obvious to God, especially on days when I want to have a candy bar and
he would rather I had serenity.)

I used to hide to escape, but this is different.
Being hidden in God creates a healthy, safe place.
Here I talk, trust, and feel without the drivenness.
Here I find acceptance and love. I can tell when I have
stepped out of my hiding place because the driven-
ness begins. When I see it happening, I retreat.

*Thank you, God, for allowing me to hide
myself in you.*

I align my thoughts and desires
with God's.

# Forgiving Those I Fear

*Bear with each other and forgive whatever
grievances you may have against one
another. Forgive as the Lord forgave you.*
—COLOSSIANS 3:13

Forgiveness can be scary. If I release my resentments, I make myself vulnerable to be hurt again. The people I resent probably aren't going to change, so how will I protect myself from them? What will I do when they trample my boundaries again by insulting me, ignoring me, or hurting me?

I ask God to be my protector. When I face the people I fear, I ask God to intervene and remind me of my worth in him, to remind me of the truth about myself if they tell lies about me, and to remind me that he loves me as they are unable to do.

Only when I believe that God is my protector can I forgive.

*Please, God, help me forgive those I fear.
Stand between them and me as a strong and
sturdy guardian angel.*

God can provide the protection I need
to help me forgive others.

# Rich Reading

*Let the word of Christ dwell in you richly.*
—COLOSSIANS 3:16A

My prayer and meditation life can get airy and meaningless when I'm not making concrete contact with God by reading the words he has placed on earth for me. I understand the Bible to be his love letter to me so that I may stand in the confidence that I am loved. It helps me know God's will for me.

Reading Scripture also keeps my relationship with God from becoming one-sided with me talking to him all the time. I want to hear God's input about my life.

I want to read about the struggles of those who have gone before me and how they overcame their personal character defects. I want to see how unlikely people such as Moses (an escaped convict), Rahab (a prostitute), and Matthew (an extortionist) became useful to God. This reassures me that there is hope for me!

*God, help me reorganize and be receptive
to what you are saying to me through
your word.*

I can sense the love of God and know
his true character as I read about him
in the Bible.

# *Pleasing God*

*We are not trying to please men but God,
who tests our hearts.*—1 THESSALONIANS 2:4

What does it take to quit trying to please people
so much? It happens only when I find someone more
important to please. Surrendering my character defects to God is teaching me to please him first. My
conscience nudges me daily, asking, "Who are you
trying to please now?" Gradually I change my people-
pleasing behaviors until I care less and less about
what others think.

Slowly my desires are beginning to coincide
with God's enough that I can try to please myself. As
I quiet the drivenness inside me, I trust my instincts
and intuition and I feel comfortable with the choices
I make.

*God, I am grateful that my simple growth
pleases you and that you teach me to please
the best parts of myself.*

Seeking God's approval first dissolves my
people-pleasing ways.

# Grateful Anyway

*. . . give thanks in all circumstances,*
*for this God's will for you in Christ Jesus.*
—1 THESSALONIANS 5:18

I'm good at listing for God the things I would like to have that he isn't providing. I see what others around me have or I see what I could have—and I want all of it!

Being thankful for what I have means that I trust that God provides exactly what I need. If I needed one more thing, one more friendship, one more success, he would provide it.

If I ask God for something and he doesn't give it to me, I trust that he has a good reason. Perhaps there's a wiser path to what I want. After all, when I begged for relief from my eating disorder, he didn't miraculously free me. He put me on a path of growth and struggle. I will emerge a much wiser person for doing it his way.

*I thank you, God, for all my circumstances,*
*even the ones that baffle and hurt me.*
*I trust you in these circumstances.*

Gratefulness relieves my inner neediness.

# *Taking Financial Responsibility*

*. . . we were not idle when we were with you, nor did we eat anyone's food without paying for it.*—2 THESSALONIANS 3:7–8

Now that I'm abandoning my magical thinking, I see that most "free" things aren't free. I may get a free dinner for watching a presentation, but I pay the price of resisting the presenter's pressure tactics. Wasn't that part of the deal? Didn't I agree to be pressured (have my boundaries violated!) so I could have a free dinner?

Since my abstinence and recovery are rooted in a clear conscience, I can no longer afford to get something for nothing. I can't let the same person take me out to lunch over and over without paying her back in some way. I don't try to get a good deal from a friend; if anything, I want to pay my friend well. I keep relationships from being tainted by taking responsibility for my own finances and resources.

*Stop me, God, before I run up debts to people who love me.*

Paying my way is less expensive in the long run.

# *Cutting Corners?*

*Be diligent in these matters; give yourself
wholly to them, so that everyone may see
your progress.*—1 TIMOTHY 4:15

When I scoop out my portion from the serving
dish, how I want to help myself to a more than generous portion! As I finish that first helping, I want to
change my abstinence and decide that two helpings
are permissible. And when I arrive at a party, I suddenly wish that my abstinence included a handful of
M & Ms and roasted almonds at parties.

Changing my abstinence on the spur of the
moment is a subtle way of saying that I don't trust
God to provide me with the physical sustenance and
emotional support I need. A prayerfully considered
abstinence that is not too strict or too lenient can be
a powerful tool only if I diligently follow it.

When my abstinence gets sloppy, I admit to God
that I'm not trusting him and I ask him to help me
trust him more.

*God, give me more diligence in following
the abstinence I have chosen.*

Cutting corners on my abstinence shows
that I need to trust God in more of my life.

# *Simply Content*

*But godliness with contentment is great gain.*
*For we brought nothing into this world, and*
*we can take nothing out of it. But if we have*
*food and clothing we will be content with*
*that.*—1 TIMOTHY 6:6–8

My personal neediness has convinced me to make a big deal out of everything. If I'm shopping, I must buy too much. If I'm looking for a place to live, it must be the best. If I'm eating a meal (even in my abstinence), it must include all my favorite foods. I used to think this would make me happy.

Godliness with contentment means that I can be happy with a simple lifestyle. I can enjoy simple pleasures such as taking walks with friends, curling up with a book, and playing volleyball. I don't have to outdo anyone or prove anything to anyone.

I know I am loved by God and by many other people. I know that I'm growing. I know that even when I don't know exactly what's going on, I have the tools to survive.

*God, place in me a love for simplicity*
*to fuel my recovery.*

When I keep it simple, I can make it.

# Malignant Obsession

*For the love of money is a root of all kinds
of evil.*—1 TIMOTHY 6:10

When my peace and happiness revolve around a
thing, it absorbs and betrays me and puts me on the
brink of various kinds of evil. When I am obsessed
with food and thinness, it becomes poison to me.
When I watch too much television, I don't listen to
my family and friends. When I am hooked on my
career, I confuse making a living with making a life.

I can find balance by copying the attitudes of
mature people around me. As I get used to the feeling
of balance, I get better at detecting the drivenness
when it first appears. Even before I feel the thunder
of it, I talk to someone about it. I become accountable for it. I release the thing before it becomes an
obsession.

*Teach me, God, to sense my drivenness and
face it before it takes over.*

I love people and use things instead of
loving things and using people.

# *Assertiveness*

*For God did not give us a spirit of timidity,
but a spirit of power, of love and of self-
discipline.*—2 TIMOTHY 1:7

Recovering from my eating disorder has helped
me stand up for myself. Instead of indulging in fear,
I ask God for power; instead of indulging in selfishness, I ask God for love; instead of indulging in
laziness, I ask God for self-discipline. It was those
feelings of fear, selfishness, and laziness that con-
tributed to my need to eat.

As I surrender each of these defects to God, I'm
not so needy and I can assert myself more. The love
and self-discipline I'm learning help me balance my
assertiveness so that I'm neither inappropriately ag-
gressive nor shy and withdrawn.

Life isn't as scary and confusing as it once was.

*Thank you, God, for giving me this spirit of
power, love, and self-discipline.*

I can not only face food, but I can also
assert myself in appropriate ways.

# *Making Peace*

*Don't have anything to do with foolish and stupid arguments, because you know they produce quarrels.*—2 TIMOTHY 2:23

I argue in many different ways. Sometimes I work so hard to prove my point that I alienate others in the process. Other times, I nitpick because someone is talking about my pet peeve or a celebrity I don't like. Still other times a restless grouchiness creeps up within me. It's like a lion I can't tame, and it makes me itch to start a squabble. I feel as if nothing that anyone does is right.

Now I know that serenity is an option. I can choose to get away and journal, pray, or talk to someone. I can take a walk or a shower and release it. I can state my position and be done with it. I can agree to disagree and feel at peace, even though everyone doesn't agree with me—even if no one agrees with me.

*God, help me choose peace when I feel cantankerous.*

It takes two to quarrel, and I choose not to participate.

# *Resentments*

*And the Lord's servant . . . must be kind to
everyone, able to teach, not resentful.*
—2 TIMOTHY 2:24

My resentments are some of the many precious
things I am surrendering to God. Some of them have
been with me a long time, and I have nursed them
and kept them healthy. It's as if they are long-time
companions.

But nurturing these resentments chained me to
my compulsion. Resenting people and circumstances
made me grouchy, gossipy, and negative. These feelings made me want to compulsively eat, purge, or
starve. Because of them, I have hurt people and limited my growth severely.

Listing these resentments is freeing me from
bondage. I let go, I make amends, and I feel freed to
have a generous attitude toward others.

*God, help me to be willing to surrender my
known resentments to you.*

Resentments keep me in bondage.

# *Defensiveness Falls Away*

*To the pure, all things are pure, but to those
who are corrupted and do not believe
nothing is pure.*—TITUS 1:15

I have been so quick to judge myself without
mercy that I tend to think others are judging me, too.
I have assumed that others were attacking me, or I've
taken comments personally that were not intended
to hurt me. At times I have even been a commando in
these relationships, making quick, destructive raids
against those I perceived as my enemy.

As I recover from my eating disorder, my self-
esteem is growing. I feel more loved by God and others. This enables me to accept people's words at face
value. I have fewer misunderstandings with people.

I become more positive, too; even intentional
insults sometimes go over my head and I don't rush
in to defend myself. This is one more facet of serenity.

*God, help me sense your protection
of me so soundly that I lay down my
weapons of defense.*

Purity of thoughts can be my best defense.

# *People Pushing*

> *I would have liked to keep him with
> me. . . . But I did not want to do anything
> without your consent, so that any favor
> you do will be spontaneous and not forced.*
> —PHILEMON 13, 14

Sometimes I want something so badly that I feel like pushing others so I can have it. I want to change someone's mind, so I try to persuade them with reason after reason. I want to be chosen for a certain task, and I launch a self-promotion campaign. I want a friend to hurry up and get through the pain of her divorce because it hurts too much to be with her.

But I have come to believe that pushing violates people's boundaries. When I try to force and convince, I'm acting as if God were off somewhere sleeping and not doing his part. When I push and shove, I'm refusing to respect the other person. I'm acting as if I know much more than they know, and they would be much better off if they just listened to me. That's the same grandiosity that fuels my eating disorder. It must go.

> *Help me, God, respect others enough so
> I don't interfere with their choices
> and decisions.*

When I force the issue, I know it's time
to surrender—again!

# *Believing in Others*

*Confident of your obedience, I write to you,
knowing that you will do even more than
I ask.*—PHILEMON 21

Being a friend to people who are struggling with
eating disorders is teaching me the power of having
confidence in others. At times I have more confidence in these friends than they have in themselves.
I can challenge them, recite their strengths, smile
confidently, and say, "I believe that you can do this.
You've got a lot going for you, so why don't you give
it a try?"

That doesn't mean I'll be disappointed or proven
wrong if they fail in some way. I haven't expected that
they'll be perfect, only that they would try.

It feels risky to trust others so much, but when
I look at the progress God is making with me, nothing seems impossible!

*God, help me reflect to others some
of the confidence you have in me.*

When confidence is shared,
it can be multiplied.

# A Down-to-Earth Savior

*For we do not have a high priest who is*
*unable to sympathize with our weaknesses,*
*but we have one who has been tempted*
*in every way, just as we are—yet was*
*without sin.*—HEBREWS 4:15

Jesus Christ knows the drivenness within me and how I battle it. At some point he felt driven toward food, and he felt driven toward appearing attractive to others. He sympathizes with me and does not belittle my struggle. He understands that I can sincerely profess to love him but still love food and thinness.

Since Christ was tempted in every way, he knows temptations I will never know. In that sense, he is more human than I am. He is fully human, but still fully God.

So what? Let us then approach the throne of grace with confidence. . . . (Heb. 4:16) This means I can admit anything to God. I don't need to pray, "God, you've probably never heard this before, but. . . . He's heard it, he's seen it, he (through Christ) was tempted to do the same thing, and he understands me.

*Thank you, God, for removing my shame by*
*understanding me, knowing me, and loving me.*

I can come to God with all my neediness
and my baggage and say, "This is me.
Please love me. Please help me."

# *Suffering is OK*

*Although he [Jesus] was a son, he learned obedience from what he suffered, and, once made perfect, he became the source of eternal salvation for all who obey him.*—HEBREWS 5:8

Pretending to be fine, OK, even wonderful, is another cultural and religious practice I am trying to shed. If Jesus suffered, so will I. If he had to learn obedience, so do I.

It is not a sign of weakness or ineptness if I go through crises or if I experience pain. Having a perfect, pain-free existence is not a sign that God is working in my life.

As I cooperate with the suffering and brokenness God allows me to experience, I find empowerment and direction. As I admit my struggles, others open up to me and I see that I can help them better by listening and understanding their struggle than by rattling off formulas and advice. People used to be afraid of that old me that appeared to be so together, but they connect better with the new me who admits brokenness.

*Keep me transparent before others, God,
and help me shed that mask of looking good.*

When I show myself for the broken person
I am, God uses me most.

# *Accountable to Witnesses*

*Therefore since we are surrounded by such a
great cloud of witnesses, let us throw off
everything that hinders and the sin that so
easily entangles, and let us run with
perseverance the race marked out for us.*
—HEBREWS 12:1

When my eating disorder and defects of character entangle me, I have only one choice. I make myself accountable to a sponsor or a friend. This is my "great cloud of witnesses." I promise to call one of them when I am tempted to eat candy bars for lunch or put down my coworker.

There is power in accountability. The power doesn't come from my fearing that if I stray, these witnesses won't love me or will be disappointed in me. The power comes from breaking my isolation and joining a team. As I walk through the day and meet my problems, I have a strong sense that these others are present with me. Because of their strength, I don't become entangled again. Their example, their love for me, their determination fills in where mine falls away.

*Thank you, God, for friends I can trust
and how they help me untangle myself.*

Nothing beats teamwork.

# Too Dependent on Others

*. . . God has said, "Never will I leave you; never will I forsake you."*—HEBREWS 13:5

Only God can promise never to leave me, although I try to extract this promise from my spouse, relatives, and friends. I don't come out and say this, of course, but I expect these people who love me to never move away, to never be occupied with anyone else, to never miss an intuitive cue that I am lonely and need them.

As I maintain conscious contact with God more often and understand that he is the only one who will never leave me, I can accept the normal distractedness of those I love. I can love these people without making heavy demands on their time or violating their privacy. I can lower my expectations of them and thank them for whatever encouragement and companionship they are able to give.

*God, help me not to expect from others the kind of comfort and companionship that comes only from you.*

I can be a better friend when God is my chief friend.

# *These Truths Were Made for Walking*

*Do not merely listen to the word, and so deceive yourselves. Do what it says.*
—JAMES 1:22

Learning the truth about compulsive eating and dieting isn't enough. Talking to others about my feelings isn't enough. I have to follow through. As I meet each obstacle in life, I can surrender my will. I can confront my negative thoughts with the truth that I am valued and loved by God.

What if I am too rebellious or too lazy to pursue recovery today? Should I give up?

No, I can pray to be willing to be willing. I can do everything that I am willing to do. Others may even lose their patience with me, but when I ask God to release in me a willingness, I know it will happen.

*God, help me to be willing to give up whatever is blocking my progress.*

Power is found as I turn each obstacle over to God.

# *Being Right Isn't Enough*

*Mercy triumphs over judgment!*—JAMES 2:13

There's more to life than being right. God is the best proof of that. He is perfectly right, but even better, he is perfectly merciful. Even though I deserve judgment, he suspends judgment and lets mercy win.

Can I suspend judgment? Do I have to be right all the time? Can I overlook the faults of others? Can I give others a break?

Being right used to feel so good. Now, showing mercy feels even better. Mercy goes beyond judgment. It fills the gap between the flawed persons that people are and the perfect persons God intends for them to be. I can look at the negative facts in a situation, but temper my conclusions with mercy. I feel closer to my father God when I imitate him this way.

*Help me, God, show mercy to the people
I have been harsh with.*

Love surpasses rightness.

# *Envy Comes Knocking*

*For where you have envy and selfish
ambition, there you find disorder and every
evil practice.*—JAMES 3:16

On some days the grass looks greener everywhere else but in my yard. This person is thinner,
that one is more attractive, another one makes more
money. When I feel envious, I dislike people I don't
even know and wish the worst on people I do know.

To set aside envy, I remember the importance of
having character instead of possessions. I look at how
far God has brought me. He didn't create me to be all
things to all people, but to fulfill the purposes he is
revealing to me. I find contentment in continuing to
discover those purposes, and I'm learning to enjoy
watching others discover theirs.

*God, help me focus on what you've given me
to do, and help me to be thankful for the
help and achievements of others.*

When I'm at peace with who I'm
becoming, I'm free from envy.

# *Resisting the Enemy*

*Submit yourself, then, to God. Resist the devil,
and he will flee from you.*—JAMES 4:7

My spiritual enemy deceives me with lies. These
lies wage war on my mind:

- You will always look stupid.
- You will never get anywhere in life.
- No one really likes you.

I resist this enemy by speaking the truth back
and renouncing the lies:

- My body isn't perfect, but God loves me as I
  am. I am satisfied with the way I look.
- I am cooperating with God to achieve what he
  wants me to achieve.
- Some people like me, and I'm thankful for that.

I resist this enemy most effectively when I re-
nounce his lies and continue surrendering myself
to God.

*God, help me recognize the enemy's lies and
speak the truth aloud.*

I am responsible for speaking the truth to
counteract the enemy's lies.

# Giving Up My Defects of Character

*Humble yourselves before the Lord, and he will lift you up.*—JAMES 4:10

It's one thing to admit my character defects of self-pity and rage, but it's another to give them to God. To be honest, I need them. I've used them to survive. How will I get anyone's attention if I don't feel sorry for myself, fly into a rage, or try to impress them? Will I cease to exist to others?

Sometimes it is hard to be willing to get rid of them. I have to let go of all the controls, the neediness, and the attempts to patch myself up. I can lean on the seemingly ridiculous idea that God will rescue me once I quit rescuing myself.

This doesn't sound like humility, but that's what it is. It's admitting powerlessness. It's admitting that I'm a flawed human being, and that only God is powerful enough to heal me.

*God, I admit my powerlessness to you once again and ask you to lift my defects of character from me.*

To admit powerlessness is a step of humility.

# *Hearing God's Spontaneous Will*

*Now listen, you who say, "Today or tomorrow we will go to this or that city, spend a year there, carry on business and make money."*
*. . . Instead, you ought to say, "If it is the Lord's will, we will live and do this or that."*—JAMES 4:13, 15

I used to be so smart! I had my life planned, my friends' lives planned, and my parents' lives planned. Each vacation was the playing out of a well-rehearsed plot. That control was necessary either to practice my eating disorder or to try to stop it. I was spontaneous sometimes—but only to act out my eating disorder. It ruled everything!

As I'm growing less needy, I experience the new thrills of a normal, healthy spontaneity. Life is more fun, and I don't feel guilty all the time. As I dismantle my control tower attitude, I hear God speaking to me more clearly. I hear him speaking to me through friends, family, and my better impulses. I now have the freedom to follow them.

*Help me listen to you, God, instead of my own efforts to control.*

I listen to God's will as it is revealed to me.

# Coming Clean

*Therefore, confess your sins to each other
and pray for each other so that you may
be healed.*—JAMES 5:16

Confessing my faults to others was one of the missing elements of my faith. Now I find cleansing and empowerment in admitting to other human beings the exact nature of my wrongs. I make no excuses, and I present myself in a transparent way: I binged; I am jealous of my friend; I fear the worst in this and every situation.

Instead of embarrassing others, I find this fresh honesty relieves them. Since they know how flawed I am, they feel free to tell me their faults. Our confessions bond us together in a powerful way.

Our mutual honesty also emblazons their struggles on my mind, and I find myself praying for them spontaneously. As part of their team, I ask God to help them in their desire for progress.

*God, give me the courage to be honest about
who I am and what I do.*

Confessing and praying with others makes
me part of a healing team.

# A Clear Conscience Under Slander

*. . . keeping a clear conscience, so that those who speak maliciously against your good behavior in Christ may be ashamed of their slander.*—1 PETER 3:16

When office gossip spread about me, when someone accused me, and when I was misrepresented, I thought about eating or starving. But now that I'm clearing my conscience, I feel less driven when this happens. I don't need to defend myself and prove myself right, because my conscience is clear. I still feel hurt, but I don't feel that old inner craziness.

If the slander continues, I have to work hard to keep my thoughts and behavior clear of resentment. Daily I have to surrender my feelings of revenge and my potential sarcastic defense speeches. At times I call a friend and become accountable. When I manage to keep this clear conscience, I find one more facet of serenity in the midst of my chaotic world.

*God, help me keep a clear conscience so I may have peace when others slander me.*

My clear conscience helps my behavior speak in my behalf when others slander me.

# *Sharing What I Have*

> *If anyone speaks, he should do it as one*
> *speaking the very words of God. If anyone*
> *serves, he should do it with the strength God*
> *provides, so that in all things God may be*
> *praised through Jesus Christ.*—1 PETER 4:11

As I heal from the inside out, I can cancel any hidden agenda in my speech or service. I serve as God leads me, not to impress, control, or manipulate.

I can't give a sales speech to those who ask me questions about eating disorders either. I share my strength, hope, and experience, and then I shut my mouth. I listen carefully, showing inquirers the love and respect they may not have shown themselves in years.

And when pastors, therapists, or doctors quiz me, I boldly share my experience with these experts, too. I'm careful to listen to my motives and try to get a sense of what God is or is not leading me to say. I don't have to dazzle anyone; I can be myself.

> *God, lead me to do and say what is your will*
> *for me today.*

I can't change anyone's thinking, but I can pass the love along that I have received.

DAY 356

# *Doubting My Progress*

*Be self-controlled and alert. Your enemy the
devil prowls around like a roaring lion
looking for someone to devour.*—1 PETER 45:8

When I blow it by eating outside my abstinence,
panicking about the future, or becoming upset about
small things, I doubt that I've changed at all. I berate
myself by asking myself if I should be doing better. I
ask myself if I am really making any progress.

It's one thing to be in recovery and another to
believe it. My spiritual enemy tries to convince me
that I am hopeless: I'll never become abstinent; I'll
never feel comfortable in life.

I can read my journals and talk to friends I've
known for years to reaffirm that yes, I've changed. I
rehearse the fact that recovery from an eating disorder is a process, and I'm still growing.

*God, help me walk in the truth that I am
progressing in my recovery.*

I can quiet the old, negative thinking that
wants to erase the progress I've made.

# How Am I Progressing?

*. . . make every effort to add to your faith goodness, and to goodness, knowledge . . . self-control . . . perseverance . . . godliness . . . brotherly kindness . . . love. For if you possess these qualities in increasing measure, they will keep you from being ineffective and unproductive. . . .* —2 PETER 1:8

How do I evaluate my progress? Are comparisons unhealthy? Most of them are, but I can compare myself now with:

- what I used to be like. Are my eating habits and character strengths growing and changing even in small ways? Do I find it slightly easier to do the right thing, love others, and stick it out in tough situations?

- what I could be like now without recovery. If my eating disorder had continued to progress, would I be miserable, much more overweight, or even dead?

- what Christ is like. What Christlike qualities do I need to possess? How am I possessing them in increasing measure?

Progress in these areas indicates that God's work in me is moving along.

*Thank you for the work you do within me.*

I evaluate my recovery by the progress
I'm making.

# *God, the Rescuer*

*. . . the Lord knows how to rescue godly men
from trials. . . .*—2 PETER 2:9

God rescues me from the clutches of midnight-pizza runs, slippery situations, and intimidating people. As I take a daily inventory every night, I can say, "Can you believe I left the drugstore without an ice cream cone? Was that really me?"

Recalling God's excellent track record of rescues gives me courage for the future and helps me depend on him even more. When I find myself overwhelmed at a party full of sweets or an all-you-can-eat salad bar, I can know that God is one step ahead of me. I don't tempt him to rescue me, but I know that if I really need it he will intervene in some way. Then it's my turn to choose to accept his intervention.

*Help me, God, recall those moments
in which you have rescued me.*

God proves to me every day that he can
restore me to sanity.

# *Denial*

*If we claim to be without sin, we deceive
ourselves and the truth is not in us.*
—1 JOHN 1:8

Denying I have a problem feeds my eating disorder and makes it grow. "It's not unusual to . . . ," I'm tempted to say.

Even though I admit my powerlessness and surrender it to God, there are other things I can be in denial about. To whom do I really need to make amends? What unhealthy habits am I holding on to? Am I still behaving compulsively about eating, even though I am abstinent?

My denial shows in different ways. I refuse to consider a criticism. I push away the thought of becoming accountable for an unhealthy habit. I make excuses for spending too much or working too hard when it's really my neediness driving me.

I know the relief that comes from turning these things over to God, so I begin by talking these things over with him.

*God, please show me my blind spots.*

It's when I think I've arrived that
I'm in trouble.

# Never-Ending Forgiveness

*If we confess our sins, he is faithful and just
and will forgive us our sins and purify us
from all unrighteousness.*—1 JOHN 1:9

God promises to forgive my sins no matter what. He doesn't say, "Wait a minute. You have three sins too many this month. Go to the back of the line." He is willing, waiting, and watching for me to come to him and confess my sins so he can forgive me.

This simple access to God and his ready forgiveness make it a little easier for me to make a habit of confessing wrongs as soon as they occur. Sometimes I wait until the end of the day or longer, but I like to turn around immediately and say, "Did you see what I just did, God?" Then I ask his forgiveness, I ask the other person's forgiveness, and I correct the situation.

As confessing to God becomes an immediate habit, I become free to change my behaviors. I'm so glad. It's about time.

*God, thank you that you so generously
forgive when I ask.*

Some things are better left said.

# *God's Love*

*How great is the love the Father has lavished
on us, that we should be called children of
God!*—1 JOHN 3:1

I keep forgetting that God loves me with a determined and relentless love. God resembles parents who watch with delight as their baby attempts to scoot and roll toward them. They smile and pick up the baby and feed their little one. God doesn't wait for me to do something spectacular before he picks me up. It's enough that I exist.

This love is not stingy. He lavishes it on me and lets me know that there's more where that came from.

And God's love gives me value; I am worth a great deal in his eyes. His love gives me strength; he will sustain me even though it looks as if everything's against me. His love gives me hope; he will help me find a way to accomplish what needs to be done.

*God, don't let me lose sight of your
great love for me.*

God is making me a complete person
by loving me.

# *Demanding Love*
# *—My Way*

*. . . God is love. This is how God showed his love among us: He sent his one and only Son into the world that we might live through him.*—1 JOHN 4:8–9

I have mistakenly assumed that God didn't love me because he didn't do everything I asked him to do—especially giving me a smooth, easy life and a perfect, attractive body. I see now that God's love goes much deeper. He does what is best for me no matter how much it costs him.

I make the same mistake with other people—I assume they don't love me unless they do everything I ask them to do. I'm learning to let people show their love in their own way. If I really love them, I won't try to control them by telling them exactly how to prove their love or loyalty to me. I will let them decide that and accept it graciously.

Like God, they may come up with ways much better than I would have prescribed. That can be delightful!

*Help me, God, accept other people's love graciously as you're teaching me to do with you.*

Demanding love in certain forms robs me and others of the joy of love.

# *Fears and Realities*

*There is no fear in love. But perfect love drives out fear, because fear has to do with punishment. The one who fears is not made perfect in love.*—1 JOHN 4:18

I fear most things. I fear failure and success. I fear rejection and intimacy. I fear looking unattractive and looking attractive. I fear that others are looking at me, and I fear they aren't looking at me. I fear that I disappoint authority figures, and I fear disappointing those who view me as an authority figure.

I'm learning to accept these realities:

- Failures, successes, and disappointments happen to everyone. They are not punishments; they are part of reality. They happen whether or not I fear them.

- God will not forsake me. He will stand by me as I walk through each struggle.

- The more I surrender my fears, the less real they become.

*God, help me feel confident in your powerful love.*

I have not been condemned to live my life in fear.

# Fear of Intimacy

*. . . I hope to visit you and talk with you face
to face, so that our joy may be complete.*
—2 JOHN 12

Receiving a letter as bold and loving as this one
from the apostle John would make me wish for an
airline strike to keep him away. Could I stand being
with someone who liked me that much?

Even though I'm beginning to understand that
God values me, I still fear intimacy with others. I'm
afraid that if wise, discerning people get close to me,
they'll discover that I'm an uneasy, frightened person.
Certainly they'll reject me! What if we eat together—
will they watch how I eat?

But living one day at a time, I can concern myself
only with whom I face today and absorbing the love
and intimacy they may offer (if any). I can focus on
what it means to give to another person and stop
worrying about how well I'm being perceived. I can
stop analyzing their behavior and start being myself.

*Thank you, God, that people care about me
enough that I find intimacy scary.
Help me to relax.*

To be loved is to be vulnerable—I'm
getting used to that.

# *Yes, I Am Thirsty*

*The Spirit and the bride say, "Come!" And let
him who hears say, "Come!" Whoever is
thirsty, let him come, and whoever wishes,
let him take the free gift of the water of life.*
—REVELATION 22:17

I keep thinking that God wants me to be good enough before he can do anything with me. When I'm good, he'll help me. When I'm perfect, he'll like me.

I'm learning that I don't have to be good enough. All I have to do is be willing. When he says, "Come!" I say, "Yes." No matter how many times I fall, I can get back up again.

I can make my neediness work *for* me instead of against me. My neediness says that I am "whoever is thirsty," and "whoever wishes." With all my brokenness in front of me, I am a prime candidate to be one who surrenders myself and says, "Yes, I will come!"

*I shed my shame and I come to you.*

When I surrender, I'm doing
what God wants.

# *Recovery Words*

**Abstinence**—A more normal eating plan of my own chosing, often three simple meals a day.

**Accountability**—Making a commitment to try to practice a healthy behavior or abstain from a compulsive one, such as overeating or throwing up.

**Amends**—Doing whatever it takes to repair insults or injuries, such as improving my attitudes, correcting my errors, or making financial restitution.

**Boundaries**—Limits or choices I make about time, privacy, familiarity, talents, or anything that defines who I am. I set up healthy boundaries about what I say, what I do, and how closely I identify myself with others. If I don't respect these things in others, I "cross" their boundaries.

**Confidentiality**—Not revealing to anyone what is shared in support-group meetings or in private conversations with recovering friends. It also includes maintaining the anonymity of other recovering persons by not mentioning their involvement in a support group.

**Conscious Contact with God**—Doing whatever I can to communicate with God on a regular basis.

**Cycle of Compulsive Behavior**—

- preoccupation (thinking about compulsive eating, dieting, purging, or starving)
- ritualization (behavioral patterns I use just before I compulsively eat, diet, purge, or starve)

- compulsive behavior (various forms of severe dieting, overeating, purging, or starving)
- despair (feeling shame and hopelessness for repeating the pattern)

**Defects of Character**—Flaws that cause me to feel needy, such as self-pity, resentment, laziness, hostility, or fear of rejection.

**Denial**—Refusing to see my faulty attitudes and behaviors, including not admitting that I have an eating disorder or that I'm angry or upset.

**Eating Disorder**—Compulsive eating, compulsive dieting, bulimia (binging and purging), or anorexia (self-starvation).

**Inventory**—A process of examining my past and present to discover the history and patterns of my eating disorder and my defects of character. This is often done thoroughly in written form one or more times and then informally at the close of each day.

**Journaling**—Writing my thoughts and feelings as honestly as possible.

**No-Crosstalk Rule**—A common method of Twelve-Step groups and some other support groups in which I may not interrupt others when they are sharing, even to ask questions or offer comfort.

**Recovery**—The process of giving up my drivenness for compulsive behavior and the behavior itself and growing into a whole person who knows and loves God.

**Sponsor**—A partner who has more recovery than I do and who can support me and warn me if I'm getting off track; someone to whom I can be accountable and know that I will be accepted.

Support-Group Meetings—Safe places in which honest feelings can be shared without threat of rejection; these include Twelve-Step meetings such as Overeaters Anonymous.

Tools—Methods and sources for enhancing my recovery such as reading recovery literature, prayer, Scripture reading, meditation, journaling, abstinence, attending support-group meetings, working with a sponsor, and writing an inventory.

# *Spiritual Growth Words*

God's Grace—God's generous willingness to give me what I need, not what I deserve.

Justified—When God removes my blame and guilt and declares me right in his eyes.

For more information on recovery from compulsive eating, see *When Food Is Your Best Friend* by Jan Johnson, HarperSanFrancisco.

# Index